THE SILENT FILM UNIVERSE

BY
BEN MODEL

UNDERCRANK PRODUCTIONS LLC

NEW YORK, NY

THE SILENT FILM UNIVERSE

Copyright © 2025 by Ben Model

All rights reserved.

Published in the United States by:

Undercrank Productions LLC
New York, NY
undercrankproductions.com

Cover design by Marlene Weisman

ISBN: 979-8-9875546-0-9 (Paperback)
ISBN: 979-8-9875546-1-6 (Hardback)

Library of Congress Control Number: 2025900431
LC record available at https://lccn.loc.gov/2025900431

DEDICATION

To my parents, Alice and Alan Model,
whose encouragement and support
of my passion for silent movies have meant
more than words can express.

CONTENTS

Acknowledgements   i

Foreword   v
Introduction   ix

1. Motion Picture Film, and What It Can
   and Cannot Capture   1

2. An Opportunity for a Storytelling Shorthand   11

3. Silent Film's Accomplice: Your Right Brain   21

4. Silent Film's Soundscape   31

5. Iconography and Archetypes   41

6. Silent Film Leaves It Out, We Fill It In   51

7. Silent Film's Use of Text   65

8. Performance Techniques in Silent Film   79

9. The Speed(s) of Silent Film   91

10. Silent Film After the Silent Era   153

11. The Future of Silent Film   169

Epilogue   181

ACKNOWLEDGEMENTS

There are many people I wish to thank for their support, inspiration, assistance, talents, camaraderie, collaboration, and enthusiasm during the period I was working on *The Silent Film Universe* and over the years that preceded this—all of which have led to my creating this book.

First and foremost, I am forever grateful to Jeanine Basinger, Corwin-Fuller Professor Emerita of Film Studies at Wesleyan University and founder of the Wesleyan Cinema Archive. Jeanine's belief that I was someone who could create and teach a silent film course at Wesleyan changed my life. Deep thanks go also to Scott Higgins, the Charles W. Fries Professor at Wesleyan, director of the College of Film and the Moving Image, and curator of the Wesleyan Cinema Archive. Jeanine's and Scott's mentorship, friendship, and guidance—coupled with my taking students on a curated journey through the silent era every year—has allowed me to crystallize and affirm my theories about silent film as a unique medium. Thanks also go to Marc Longenecker and Richard Contrastano of Wesleyan's film department, and to all the students who have taken my "Silent Storytelling" class since 2015.

I'm thankful to my friends and colleagues who read drafts of *The Silent Film Universe*. The feedback, keen insights, and suggestions provided by Michael Abadi, Michael Hayde, David March, Jeff Rapsis, Ben Robinson, and Michael Tisserand have been invaluable. I must also thank my blog subscribers, who enthusiastically read and responded to the sixty-five posts I wrote in 2021 which became the first draft of this book.

I'm also very grateful to the people who, years ago, invited me to present my lecture on "undercranking" in silent film: Lisa Stein Haven ("Charlie in the Heartland" Chaplin conference), Rob Stone and Rachel Del Gaudio ("Mostly Lost" workshop, Library of Congress), Gerry Orlando (Syracuse Cinefest), Dave Kehr (Museum of Modern Art), Shirley Hughes (Toronto Silent Film Festival), Bill Shaffer and Denise Morrison (Kansas Silent Film Festival), and Abbey Lustgarten (Criterion Collection, Blu-ray release of *The Kid*).

Epic kudos to my very dear friends whose special talents are on display in the "production values" of this book: Marlene Weisman for her inventive and eye-popping graphic design of the cover, Rob Stone for his artful book layout, and Robert Arkus for his deft photo editing.

Thanks also go to my comrades-in-arms who have fed and enhanced my interest in silent movies and in visual and physical comedy over many years. This community of fellow enthusiasts, mavens, performers, and practitioners includes everyone listed above, as well as Bill Bowers, Serge Bromberg, Peter Bufano, Luis Caballero, David Carlyon, Hilary Chaplain, David Denton, Mike Dobson, Dino Everett, Rob Farr, Shane Fleming, Eric Grayson, Joel Jeske, Dan Kamin, Jim Kerkhoff, Crystal Kui, Bruce Lawton, Mark Lonergan, Edward Lorusso, Ron Magliozzi, Leonard Maltin, Steve Massa, Josh Mills, Jon C.

ACKNOWLEDGEMENTS

Mirsalis, Dick Monday, Anne Morra, Keith Nelson, William Perry, Thomas Reeder, Tiffany Riley, Elif Rongen-Kaynakçi, Lynanne Schweighofer, Jeff Seal, Dylan Skolnick, Ned Thanhouser, Frank Thompson, John Towsen, Brent Walker, Geo. Willeman, and Joseph Yranski.

I want to honor the memory of my mentors who have passed, whose generosity of time, knowledge, and wisdom meant the world to me. As someone who was a generation or two younger than they were, it meant so much to me to be taken under the wing of such respected elders of the silent film brain trust. I raise a glass to Walter Kerr, Lee Erwin, William K. Everson, Charles Silver, and Eileen Bowser.

Finally, and most importantly, to my family: my deepest gratitude goes to my loving parents, Alice and Alan Model, who encouraged my interest in silent film since it first captivated me as a toddler and who—along with my sister, Debbie—have always supported me in my life and my art. My deep appreciation and love go to my biggest cheerleaders, my dear wife, Mana Allen, and darling daughter, Molly Model, for their love in all ways, always.

FOREWORD

by Jeanine Basinger

I first met Ben Model in March of 2006 when I invited him to Wesleyan University in Middletown, Connecticut, to perform the live musical accompaniment for a screening of Harold Lloyd's *Safety Last* (1923). I expected a great evening, but it surpassed everything I had imagined. Ben showed up with his new virtual theatre organ, and not only played to perfection, thrilling the crowd, but also gave a wonderful lecture about the history of music for silent films and showed a set of slides shown in movie houses during the silent film era. Ben became—by popular demand—a regular visitor to our theater, and in 2015 we hired him to teach a class on silent film for which the very lucky students would have him accompanying every film screened. I am happy to say that this class still goes forward, and as of this writing, Ben Model has just presented musical accompaniment for *Street Angel* (1928) at one of our film courses.

Because of the Wesleyan connection, I have been present for Ben's work for nearly two decades. As a result, I am uniquely aware of his deep commitment to silent film and its preservation, its history, its glory, and, above all, the sheer fun it offers modern audiences. I have been privileged to have many conversations with Ben about movies. *The Silent Film Universe* is thus, to me, like a long and stimulating talk with him. As Ben "speaks" in the book, he is a musician. A scholar. An historian. A visual

v

analyst. A theorist. A member of the audience. A critic. But always, always, he is a fan. A true lover of the silent movie in all its forms. He is both erudite and funny, a questioner and an answerer. He is a discoverer of forgotten films and artists, and a passionate supporter of the known and respected. He examines single films in depth, and provides clear examples for any points he makes. He tells you many things you didn't know and clarifies and deepens the ones you did. He defines the key elements of what he feels silent films really are: "the silence, the monochrome imagery, the speed-up of action in the films being shown at a faster rate than they were shot at, and the reliance on the audience's imagination or 'right brain' as an unwitting collaborator in the storytelling. These elements—combined with group experience of being in the audience, along with the live musical accompaniment— are what silent cinema truly is." Ben Model's provocative up-front observation is: "silent film's silence, oddly enough, is possibly its greatest asset."

In *The Silent Film Universe*, Ben Model has written a unique book, and only he could do it. If I asked you who would be an ideal person to explain and define the art of making silent films, you might wish for Chaplin or Keaton, Griffith or Sennett, Pickford or Gish. You might say you'd want one of the behind-the-scenes innovators of the era—a writer, editor, or cinematographer—someone who understood how people who worked without sound conceived their storytelling process. What was their plan to reach their audience? You might even wish for someone from one of those audiences to tell you what it was like when they went out each day to watch movies that had no spoken dialog. There are, of course, books written by some of the people who were there in various capacities, but no one from the past can provide you with today's perspective of history, the modern analysis of reception and perception, and the definition of sound as it was performed, imagined, and indicated for an era in which it is taken for granted. Ben Model can. And does.

The Silent Film Universe is a book written by a man who lives in that universe on a daily basis, but not as a scholar alone in an ivory tower. He ventures out into the world, to museums, to movie houses, to international venues, to colleges and high schools, to small towns in obscure places, to play for audiences he does not know. While he plays, he looks up at the light on the screen, touches his keys, and provides glorious musical sound that he weds to the image. *The Silent Film Universe* could not be written by anyone else. It is the end product of Ben's experience, and it is a hands-on, imaginative, thought-provoking, and illuminating presentation on silent film.

INTRODUCTION

There isn't a time I can remember when silent movies weren't a part of my life. My mom says that I discovered Charlie Chaplin on TV when I was a toddler. I grew up during the 1960s, when silent comedies were shown on independent regional TV stations as kids' programming, and some public television stations would run them as filler.

Starting somewhere around fourth grade I went up a level. I was gifted books like *The Films of Charlie Chaplin* (1965, Citadel Press) for birthdays and holidays. I saved allowance and lawn-mowing money to buy 8mm copies of silent comedy shorts from Blackhawk Films[1] on half-price sale. I watched episodes of *The Silent Years* produced by Killiam Shows—with beautiful piano scores by William Perry—on WNET, our PBS affiliate. A paper route during high school funded more acquisitions and a bump up to Super 8mm, sometimes with sound.

Growing up in the suburbs during the pre-internet era meant that getting to see more silent film was a challenge, to say the least. It also meant I was the only person I knew who dug silent film. My fascination was difficult—impossible, really—to explain to anyone.

A unique breakthrough in my ability to see more silents occurred in middle school. The most meaningful thing about my Bar Mitzvah was one of the gifts I got. My

---

[1] Blackhawk Films, Inc. sold copies of silent and classic films to home movie enthusiasts and collectors from the 1930s to the 1980s. It continues today as The Blackhawk Films Collection, a film archive and production company.

family's friends the Feltensteins gave me an autographed copy of a brand-new book called *The Silent Clowns* by Walter Kerr (1975, Knopf), which I devoured. The following year, assigned to find a biography in the school library and write a report on it, I found a copy of *When the Movies Were Young* (1925, E. P. Dutton & Company) by Mrs. D. W. Griffith (Linda Arvidson) among the limited selection of books in the Dewey Decimal number assigned to cinema. Arvidson chronicles Griffith's career up through the making and release of *The Birth of a Nation* (1915). In discussing my book choice with me, my teacher told me I should watch the film as part of my report.

Today, you can say aloud, "I'd like to screen D. W. Griffith's *The Birth of a Nation*," and within a second or two your TV, computer, or mobile device will present you with several copies of the film. In 1975, a thirteen-year-old in Larchmont, New York, didn't have that luxury. A Super 8mm copy of the film sold by Blackhawk Films cost around $100, which was a lot more money then than it is now, especially for an eighth-grader.

My mom knew that Walter Kerr and his wife, Jean, lived in our town. Mr. Kerr was the drama critic for the *New York Times* and author of many books on the theater, and Mrs. Kerr was a playwright and humorist. She is possibly best known to classic film fans for her book *Please Don't Eat the Daisies* (1957, Doubleday), which was turned into a Hollywood movie in 1960 and then a TV sitcom (1965–67, NBC). My dad remembered hearing or having read somewhere that Walter Kerr had a large film collection. I wrote and mailed a letter to Mr. Kerr, introducing myself and letting him know of my enjoyment of his book, my deep interest in silent film, and my film-search plight. Four days later, he called, and said he'd be happy to show me the film.[2]

Over the next half dozen years—either on my own or with my friend Richard Steinberg and sometimes my younger sister Debbie—I spent many Monday evenings in Mr. Kerr's study being shown silent comedy films by the guy who literally wrote the book on them. I arrived at NYU film school having seen nearly all the feature films by Chaplin, Keaton, Lloyd, Langdon, and lesser-known comedian Raymond Griffith.

My similar interests in music and filmmaking kind of coalesced in college. I began accompanying silents on piano for film history courses at NYU taught by Robert Sklar and, especially, by William K. Everson. From the start, I made a point of finding and learning from film accompanists working in NYC. I met and befriended William Perry at MoMA, and theatre organist Lee Erwin at the Carnegie Hall Cinema. Erwin had been a movie organist in the 1920s and became both a friend and a mentor. My having Walter Kerr, William K. Everson, and Lee Erwin as people in my life who were a generation or so older than me—and who generously said "yes" to and fed my interests in silent movies—meant a great deal to me.

---

[2] When Mr. Kerr screened his 16mm print of *The Birth of a Nation* for me, in addition to talking about the film and about D. W. Griffith, he made sure to impart cultural and historical context for the film's racist content and messages.

About twenty-five years after college, I was at a point when accompanying silents became what I did for a living, full-time. I was playing for way more shows now, many of which were screenings I also introduced, and I was therefore in a dual role of aiding audiences musically while the film was onscreen, and contextualizing each film for the shows' attendees.

Introducing myself to people now as a silent film pianist—instead of as an independent filmmaker or comedian, as I'd been doing previously—I encountered everything from "Oh, cool!" to "Does anyone still show those?" and, once, "No, seriously...what do you do?" Throughout the 2010s I found myself being asked four things pretty consistently during Q&As after the films; in promotional interviews with journalists, radio and podcast hosts, and bloggers; and in social situations when people asked what I did. Three questions were easier to answer: "Was that the original score?" "Don't your hands get tired?" "How'd you get started accompanying silent movies?" There were facts, history, and my own origin story to reply with.

The fourth question was more of a challenge: "Why do you like silent film?"

I'd always do my best to explain my own interest in and passion for silent movies. There would invariably be follow-up to this, about whether there are audiences for these screenings and why I thought that was so. Trying to explain why I think silent movies appeal to today's audiences was even trickier.

Why *do* I and so many others enjoy silent movies?

Why would an entertainment form from over a hundred years ago that was replaced by another, technologically and by the public, be of any use or enjoyment today? And yet, it is…and the audience and interest in silent cinema appears to be growing every year.

You may have asked yourself these same questions or have been asked by friends or family and had the same challenges explaining it.

I've estimated that over the last fifteen years alone I've accompanied well over 2,000 silent film programs. The number of films could very well be 30 percent higher, since many of the shows were composed of shorts. Throughout all of these I went on a mindful journey to better understand what it was about silent film that wove its storytelling magic on audiences of the 1910s and 1920s as well as on those of today.

Through this process, I gradually became aware of and developed the deeper understanding of silent cinema I was after. My observations and realizations about the visual storytelling language of silent film and how it was used in an unspoken partnership with the viewer led to my regarding silent film as a unique and separate medium unto itself. There is a calculated, deliberate, and artful way that the flow of information involves leaving out some of the details. This, combined with unique performance techniques, the way title cards are used, and the ubiquitous practice of what is commonly referred to as "undercranking," allow the onscreen world of silent films' stories to inhabit an alternate plane of existence.

I call this the Silent Film Universe.

This universe that exists somewhere between reality and dream state, fusing the screen and our imagination, is why I love silent film. I believe the same applies for audiences of the past and the present, as well as those to come.

The chapters that follow lay out the natural (and unnatural) laws of the Silent Film Universe, as well as the cinematic building blocks that allowed the storytellers and creatives who were making moving pictures in the pre-talkie era to entertain audiences in a way that was (and is) only possible in a silent movie. What I outline is the medium's visual language, a unique one that developed, flourished, and became increasingly creative and inventive rather than functioning merely to compensate for the absence of sound.

Although the terms "silent film," "silent movie," and "silent cinema" are interchangeable, for the purposes of this book I will use the term "silent film" when I am referring to the *medium* of silent film. The other two are reserved for a particular film or films, or to all motion pictures made before the advent of sound film. When I use "silent film," I mean the cinematic language of the medium and the methods by which it is used to communicate and entertain. The phrase also indicates the making of these films and the decisions that were made about what would or would not be onscreen.

Examples of scenes or shot sequences from certain silent movies will be described in the chapters that follow, to illustrate the different points being made. Visit the website silentfilmmusic.com/SFUniverse to view corresponding video clips.

INTRODUCTION

Regardless of the many years I've spent accompanying silent movies, this subject will not be covered here. The purpose of a silent film's musical score is to enhance or optimize the bond between the screen and the audience or viewer, setting the mood and supporting the drama or action or comedy onscreen. The musical score is an ancillary part of the medium, even though it is an important and, in some ways, essential component to watching a silent movie. However, the accompaniment is in service of the motion picture, and it is the motion picture itself that I am concerning myself with here. In 2012 I launched *The Silent Film Music Podcast*, and its many episodes contain my thoughts on scoring silent films as well as excerpts of my live performances.

I've written *The Silent Film Universe* so that we can all have a better and deeper understanding of what the medium of silent film truly is, what it is capable of, and why — in order to get to the bottom of why we like silent movies.

1.

MOTION PICTURE FILM, AND WHAT IT CAN AND CANNOT CAPTURE

From the inception of moving pictures in the 1890s, the core, basic photochemical elements of moving pictures set its limits. The physical element of motion picture film captured and reproduced images of life, in monochromatic form, and it did so without including sound. Viewers and audiences at the time experienced, accepted, and even marveled at moving pictures in this very state, from the dawn of cinema through the end of the silent era.

The parameters for what is left to us as viewers to fill in, then and now, were also set at the dawn of the motion picture.

The leaving-out of elements of life experienced outside of moving pictures, as well as the imprecise reproduction of movement—be it "herky-jerky" or slightly faster (or both)—was intrinsic to this entertainment form. And it stayed that way until the 1930s, when what everyone up to that point called "movies" was now called "silent movies," and "movies" morphed into a new medium with the addition of sync sound and, later, full color.

The people who made moving pictures during cinema's initial few decades developed a storytelling language that danced with the fact that elements of life and reality were being excluded. This gradual evolution couldn't have been intentional or by design. There wasn't time for planning and mulling things over, because of the whopping and insatiable demand for product. People in the moving picture industry, such as it was in its nascent decade or so, were caught up in the cauldron of production and learning on the go, with a few dozen production outfits releasing multiple single and split-reel films weekly. And yet, this language development happened amid the creative maelstrom of picture-making achieving its fish-walking-on-land evolution at the tail end of the nickelodeon or "cinema of attractions" era, circa 1909 to 1913.

What I have observed in films from this time period is that the makers of screen entertainment appear to have been spurred on by the limitations of silent cinema. They moved away from a more literal, theatrical or proscenium-based depiction of their stories and instead toward eliminating bits of storytelling. People making moving pictures appear to have intuitively sensed that the way forward was in taking *more* things away from what was shown. This allowed for and enabled new, greater, and more economic levels of storytelling expression in this new entertainment medium.

Before discussing the ways in which the makers of silent cinema created and developed its cinematic language, I will lay out the main absences in silent cinema that seem, on the surface, to have been handicaps but that were just the way things were. People who made and who attended moving pictures in the nickelodeon era of the first decade of the twentieth century (which I will hereafter refer to as the 1900s or the aughts) and onward only knew this new entertainment form as a miracle of sorts, and only knew they were creating or experiencing something unique and remarkable.

•   •   •

For me, the key aesthetic elements of silent film are the silence, the monochrome imagery, the speed-up of action in the films being shown at a faster rate than they were shot at, and the reliance on the audience's imagination or "right brain" as an unwitting collaborator in the storytelling. These elements—combined with the group experience of being in the audience, along with the live musical accompaniment—are what silent cinema truly is.

Walter Kerr opens his magnificent book on silent film comedy, *The Silent Clowns*, with five chapters about the basic nature of silent movies. It is the book's entire Part I, and it establishes the lay of the land of what stage performers, circus clowns, and vaudevillians brought to cinema.[3] A cinema that was—on the surface—limited could be adapted to because of its form and because of the performers' abilities in physical performance. It was a new entertainment form that allowed these creatives to take their craft places it could not go when practiced or

---

[3] If you do not have a copy of *The Silent Clowns*, I heartily recommend you acquire one, and read through its first section: "Part I: The Silent Camera."

performed for a live audience. It was also one that opened the possibilities of venturing into the uncharted territory of wonder, going beyond merely capturing and playing back moments of life—even when staged—just as they occurred in front of the camera.

Kerr writes of what can be viewed in the rear-view mirror as technological shortcomings as being the very elements that give license to silent film to liberate itself from the factual nature of what it captures. There are basic components of reality that are removed or missing because of the moving picture element's capabilities or lack thereof.

Silent film is two-dimensional. It lacks the full color spectrum. And the basic element of the cut elides space and time to move the viewer from one scene or story element to another.

There was no way around this. Film is flat, both film itself and the screen it is projected or viewed on. Life is three-dimensional; film and its projected image are not. That's one element of reality gone.

There were several experiments with color processes during the silent era, but for the first few decades of cinema—even when tinting was employed—movies were in black-and-white. There goes another element of reality.

The edit is what brought moving pictures beyond depiction of actualities seen in a Kinetoscope machine.[4] The time and space leaps of the edit were minimal in moving

---

[4] Edison's Kinetoscope, a coin-operated machine with a peephole viewer, was in use primarily during the mid-1890s. Kinetoscope films lasted anywhere from twenty seconds to around one minute.

pictures of the first several years of the 1900s, akin to scene breaks in a play or chapters in a novella. But once filmmakers realized you could make a story leap, visually, and the audience wouldn't get confused, the leaving-out of a time-and-space transition made by a cut from one thing to another became more of a broad jump. Eventually, as the silent era continued, these leaps increased in depth and frequency. There goes yet another element of reality, one that is akin to the dream state we all know.

Kerr lays out the above facets as the setup to the main leaving-out that is the key element of silent film and its namesake: its *silence*.

Perhaps because hearing is one of the five senses, the absence of sound invites our imagination to engage with the screen entertainment we are taking in. We unconsciously lean in, fill in the sound and dialog that is not present. Regardless of our own spoken language, we create the dialog based on visual cues from the screen. This aspect of silent film is entrancing in the same way old-time radio from the 1930s and 1940s is, its total absence of visuals inviting the listener to conjure them up for the screen of their mind. Just ask anyone who was around during the golden age of radio or who is a fan of it today.

• • •

The silence of silent film is also its most misunderstood or misinterpreted aesthetic. Many people assume that silent film is simply movies with no sound, hampered by its mute form.

True, the word "silent" is incredibly off-putting. Serving as the label for films made before the advent of sync sound or the industry's switching over to it *tells* you that "silent film" is movies with no sound. To this day, the biggest challenge in bringing a first-timer to a silent movie show is dragging them past the word "silent."

Mel Brooks's *Silent Movie* (1976) takes place at the time of its own making, and contains several gags that poke fun at the fact that silent movies have no sound. If anyone remembers one gag from the picture, it's the bit with Marcel Marceau.

Brooks's character, Mel Funn, a film director who wants to make a silent movie, calls up Marceau to ask him to be in the film. Cut to Marceau's flat—he is in full mime makeup and costume as his iconic character Bip. His phone ringing is indicated with a gag title— "Sonnez...sonnez...!" Marceau walks (against the wind, of course) to the phone and answers it, listens to Funn's request, and—in the only use of sync dialog in the film— says "No!"

Anyone doing an impression of old-timey silent movies will mouth words and make gestures to make fun of the fact that you can't hear anything in a silent film. The truth, however, is not so much that silent film was "on mute," technologically, but that the lack of spoken words allowed for a level of freedom of expression. The medium's mute state—due to its lack of recorded and synchronous sound—is one of three key elements that lifts the universe of silent film from the factual world we recognize.

Silent film's silence, oddly enough, is possibly its greatest asset.

• • •

When my daughter was little, she used to call films that were in black and white "all-gray"—which is more accurate than the term "black and white" and certainly more colloquial than "monochrome."

The question of whether silent film should be "all-gray" or not is one that comes up in discussions of the medium's aesthetics. It's as if the absence of full color was—like the absence of recorded, synchronized sound—a mistake or handicap that was corrected by the development of the Vitaphone or of 3-strip Technicolor. There were several attempts at sound and color from the 1890s through the late 1920s, but the lack of sound, full color, and real-time speed certainly was not off-putting to audiences of the time. If it was, motion pictures would not have been so wildly popular, nor would they have killed off vaudeville—with assistance from radio in the second half of the 1920s.

The monochrome nature of silent film is part of its language. It is another absence of reality, one that alters viewers' expectation-of-reality, lowering it significantly. This is inclusive of the use of color tinting, toning, and any combination thereof. Hand-coloring, a dye-transfer process called Handschiegl, stencil color and even two-color Technicolor are indeed closer to reality than straight "all-gray" film, but they are at least removed enough from the full spectrum to allow this facet of silent film to work.

• • •

7

Silent cinema's baked-in mute, two-dimensional, and monochromatic properties remove elements of reality we are accustomed to encountering in real life, in order to recognize and allow the decoding of what is in front of us or what we are experiencing. Motion picture film's innate recording of life—or reenactments of it—at least give us enough of our expected and familiar reality that we do, instantly, recognize.

There may be some stagecraft or careful camera placement involved, but our expectation of reality is unwittingly adjusted to take in and accept what we are shown as reality. We believe what we are shown: that Harold Lloyd is in fact hanging off the side of a building several stories up in *Safety Last* (1923), that Douglas Fairbanks would spontaneously dive over a parapet and slide down a three-story tapestry in *Robin Hood* (1922), that Mary Pickford is an orphan leading younger orphans on an escape through a swamp full of alligators in *Sparrows* (1926).

Silent film acknowledges our expectation of reality and the amount of trust we put in what we are shown, and takes advantage of this to create a different reality—the Silent Film Universe. It does so by taking advantage of our ability to recognize life's events when they are presented to us and then eliding pieces of these events, a deliberate and poetic leaving-out of details of story or physical action, giving us partial or merely suggestions of dramatic elements. Without our being aware of it happening, this process activates our imagination and our memories of life experiences to fill in what we are not shown or told.

Mary Pickford in *Sparrows* (1926). Her character's age is never mentioned in the film, and Pickford herself was around twenty-five years older than her fellow orphans. (courtesy of Robert Arkus)

•   •   •

However, for me, what makes silent film a unique medium is its skewing of reality by presenting it to us at a tempo that appears to be sped up while behaving as if it was not at all.

I don't think anyone has been as fascinated as I have been with silent film's speed-up—the fact that from some point in the early-to-mid 1910s, motion picture film was being projected in theaters at a rate that was faster than taking speed ("taking" meaning "filming"), but at the same time does not look like film that is running too fast.

Walter Kerr asserts that silent film is supposed to be projected faster than the speed at which it was filmed, and that this is one of the core elements of the medium. He

9

grew up seeing these films in theaters in the 1920s, and so had firsthand knowledge and experience of viewing silent movies this way. He gives a number of examples and bits of evidence to back up his own childhood and teenage memories.

Kerr, as an adult, had a sizable 16mm film collection. Although 16mm projectors can run at either 24 frames per second (for sound film) or 16 fps (for watching one's home movies), he always ran the silent movies at the 24 fps "sound" setting during the many times he showed me silent comedies at his home when I was in my teens and twenties.

Over the fifteen years prior to the publishing of this book, I have done research on the subject of silent films' filming and projection speeds—and continue to do so—and firmly believe that this speed-up is more than just projecting the film faster. That running silent movies faster than "real-life speed" is not a mistake, that it is authentic and proper. And, more importantly, that everyone involved in making motion pictures during the silent era knew it and accommodated it in their performances. I will cover this core aspect of what we refer to now as "undercranking" in Chapter 9 of this book. I will outline in detail what I have been able to find and understand about precisely how this overlooked and unnoticed aspect of cinematic sleight of hand in silent film worked during the making of the films...and still works today.

These are the natural laws of the Silent Film Universe, the ones that skew away from those that exist in reality.

Let's take a look at what these allow for.

2.

AN OPPORTUNITY FOR A STORYTELLING SHORTHAND

Silent film does not exist on the same plane as reality. It is its own reality—its own edition of it, anyway. There is a freedom in this existence, a freedom from a necessity to replicate reality or adhere to rules of natural laws or of time and space. It is the basic aesthetics of silent film that lift the action and story of the screen above the weight of real life.

Rather than being merely a handicapped form of cinema, as it is thought of by the uninitiated, it is actually the opposite.

Much in the same way the written word has the flexibility to express anything from meticulous fact to abstract poetry, silent film has a latitude allowing greater flexibility in storytelling and action. It is because of the things that are missing (full color range, sound) or skewed (speed) that this freedom exists. It is because the audience's imagination is a component of this screen entertainment that jumps in story and logic can be deliberately placed by the maker(s) and accepted by the viewer.

11

Silent film's unreality, alternate reality, or being unbound to reality lifts the viewer out of their experience of real life and lifts the silent filmmaker above the constraints of literal narrative, logic, and—in the case of action (gags, stunts)—even gravity itself.

Once we understand, embrace, and employ the silent film "lift" we can understand why the language of silent film is not a dead one, locked to 1900–1929, but is instead without boundaries of era and culture.

Silent film comedy in particular benefits from this combination. A certain level of logic, consequence, and sometimes laws of physics or gravity can be ignored, opening the floodgates of creativity for comedians. Walter Kerr cites a sequence of gags from the Lloyd Hamilton comedy *Move Along* (1926) to demonstrate this. The "button" on the sequence, in which Hamilton has been trying unsuccessfully to tie his shoelace while out walking, has "Ham" holding up his arm to hail something offscreen, when a streetcar enters the shot and stops. Hamilton uses one of its steps as a ledge to place his foot, ties his shoe, then calmly walks off as the streetcar pulls away—all the while, behaving like nothing is out of the ordinary about this. The conductor notices him, but hardly reacts.

Every gag in the film's shoelace-tying sequence takes place in reality, captured by the camera, but the logic and consequences of the actions and the gags are in the realm of fantasy.

They are gags that would work in a circus, vaudeville, or stage act because when we view a live performance, our imagination is activated from the moment the curtain goes up. We're not really in France or Boston, and the people we see aren't from the eighteenth or nineteenth century—we make the adjustment and go along with it.

Lloyd Hamilton in the comedy short *The Educator* (1922). Hamilton was a comedian's comedian, whose two-reel comedies included both slapstick and character-driven gags. (courtesy of Robert Arkus)

We wouldn't buy these gags or bits of business in a film with color and sync sound and real-time speed because our expectation of reality would be too great. We'd take what we're seeing as being more literal or linear. True, there are exceptions to this in sound film, but we are usually aware of a film's surreal nature or its being an homage to silent film comedy. Silent film is more of a hybrid of these two realities. It's a fusing of seeing something as it actually is while simultaneously allowing for an expanded range of possibilities. In silent film comedy,

13

gags can be more like those we associate today with animated cartoons, especially those from the late 1930s and the 1940s. The thought "But that wouldn't make sense" or "Why would she/he do *that*?" goes out the window.

If you were to take a silent film comedy short, stop after every single gag, and ask yourself, "Could I actually do this or get away with this?" or "Could this happen in real life?" you would undoubtedly find yourself saying, "Not a chance!" In making silent film comedy, the same measure of reality-checking applies and is exercised...but in the opposite direction. "Could I really *do* this?" is answered by "Who cares? Let's do it anyway." It could or should be taken as far as you can go, actually.

It's similar to what can be enacted in a clown or physical comedy routine in live performance. The audience's imagination is engaged—activated, really—and as a performer you can get away with just about anything. In silent comedy shorts of one or two reels,[5] the gag and situation could be anything it needed to be at the moment. Many comedy shorts, one-reelers in particular, play out like Dada nightmares. Two-reelers do as well, but—thanks to Chaplin's efforts to pioneer this—there is sometimes a little more emotional weight or motivation for the plot's progression.

These cartoon-esque gags are also not as grounded emotionally as they might be in a feature-length film. This is why Buster Keaton said that with features he couldn't do "impossible gags" anymore. The one place he gets

---

[5] A reel holds 1000 feet of motion picture film, and can run anywhere from nine to fifteen minutes, depending on how full the reel is and, more importantly, on the projection speed (see Chapter 9).

away with it is in *Sherlock, Jr.* (1924), but mainly because we are told that what we are watching is a dream. The surreal nightmare of *Sherlock, Jr.* is so similar to the logic and imagination in silent comedy film that when we dissolve back to reality, we as an audience have forgotten that we've been watching a dream sequence.

Galloping Bungalows (1924), a Mack Sennett comedy starring Billy Bevan and Sid Smith. The gag happening in this shot, as well as what led to this moment and what follows, could only happen in a silent film.
(courtesy of Robert Arkus)

This elasticity of logic and consequence—as well as, in some cases, the laws of gravity and physics—is what is unique and special about silent film. It's more than just dressing in 1920s clothing and performing in gesture and pantomime.

It is the very combination of recorded fact and the fantasy created by the leavings-out of silent cinema's visual language that makes the Silent Film Universe possible.

It exists in the ether of the Venn diagram overlap between the screen and our right-brain imagination. And it is this very participation by us as viewers—alone or (even better) as part of an audience—that makes silent film the universal language that it is.

This combination of taking in and decoding what we are seeing and filling in what is missing, by bringing something of our own life experience into the equation, is why these films—as old as they are—can still be understood and enjoyed by new audiences today.

•   •   •

The concept of the human brain's having left and right hemispheres was popularized in the 1960s–1970s through medical studies published in books and then in magazine articles. The basic idea was that our left brain dealt with processing logic and data and our right brain was more analytical and creative. In recent years, work has been done to debunk this through new studies and revisiting the data from the ones done half a century ago. I am aware that using the expression "right brain" throughout this book may perpetuate a neuropsychological idea that may be proved to be more myth than science. However, out of convenience, I will use the term "right brain" when referring to the brain function that synthesizes information, ideas, memories, and life experience.

•   •   •

Let's consider what we are presented with, what we are literally looking at, when we view a silent film. Because it is a purely visual medium, although aided and abetted as needed by music, it is the visual cues that give us information. This is a question I pose to elementary-school kids when I present silent film to them: "If there's no way for us to hear the actors talking, how do we know what's going on?"

The performers move in ways that help or allow us to understand the story being told to us. There's the use of facial expressions, and the use of gesture. There are intertitles giving us bits of dialog, exposition, and information about the scene we are watching.

These are the most obvious and are the answers I always get from the students. There are also the elements of film itself: photographic composition, camera placement and how close or wide the shot is, lighting, production design, and cutting.

I'm going to cover each of these aspects in detail, as there are subtleties and nuances to each. There were also developments and refinements to all of the above that occurred throughout the silent era from the early 1910s through the advent of talkies.

But one of the most important elements of silent film, perhaps one of its unique properties, is this:

There is no wasted screen time in silent film.

You can't get up to go to the bathroom, come back some minutes later, and ask your seatmate, "What'd I miss?" Not just because you'll get a scathing shushing, but because even if you (quietly) sneeze a couple of times, check your watch, or (gasp!) look at your phone, and then look back up at the screen, you've missed something. You are always being fed information, some kind of data that you need your right brain to stitch together.

• • •

One of the ways silent film economizes on storytelling information is by the dropping of non-essential bits of information in a scene. Sometimes these are at the beginning of a scene. But the general idea is to keep moving, and to keep the important dramatic beats—or comic ones—flowing.

A silent film scene is one that has had its ingredients simmered and reduced to just what is needed to convey the story's beats from the screen to our imaginations. Any extra or seemingly dead space is usually there for pacing or emotional import. But we are still being given some sort of information, either directly or by suggestion, that we fill out in our minds.

There is no fat to trim away. We are continuously engaged with the screen. It is that flow and the skipping over of elements that create the dream-state of silent film.

If someone in a silent movie travels from one location to another, we are not presented with three or four shots of them in an automobile or horse-and-carriage leaving their house, then in another location, then driving and thinking, then driving on another road, and so forth. Nor would we be presented with the sitcom convention of dissolving from one scene to a street elsewhere in the show's town or city, and then a slow pan or tilt up to the floor of an apartment building where the next scene takes place, followed by a dissolve to the next office or apartment, where the characters enter and begin the scene.

Instead, for a time-and-place transition like this in silent film we are presented with a visual equivalent of the page turn at the end of a book chapter. Usually, we are given a boost by an intertitle letting us know where our character has arrived, and maybe also giving us some information about what transpired before and after the previous scene. The title may reference other characters in the story, a passage of time, or anything else that will get us caught up and ready for what is going to happen next.

Leaving it up to us to fill in the rest.

In a silent film, no matter how great or small the leap in time, location, or story, we accept what we are told and dive right back in. In the Silent Film Universe, the depiction of life and its stories or trajectories is not literal or strictly linear. In fact, it's better when and because it isn't.

3.

SILENT FILM'S ACCOMPLICE: YOUR RIGHT BRAIN

My understanding of what silent film is revolves around the one intangible element that makes it its own medium as opposed to being a genre. It's the aspect of silent movies that is rarely spoken of, if ever. And why not? It's something we as viewers or an audience are not aware of while we're watching a silent film. It's something that happens naturally and instantly.

It's our own participation, however little or much it's employed. From the moment after a silent film's opening titles fade out and we fade in on an image, or on an expository opening title and then the film's first shot, we are—unwittingly—part of the screen experience we believe we are merely observing.

I believe that it is this innate "sound of one hand clapping" aspect of silent film, in addition to all the visually obvious components, that makes silent cinema a special, wondrous, and—dare I say, "magical"—form of film. It's one that I believe ought to be regarded as separate from sound film, and not merely thought of as old or early film because silent cinema preceded "talking pictures."

• • •

People who haven't seen or experienced silent film are always surprised to know there's an interest in it. When I show a Buster Keaton comedy short to school groups, the kids absolutely eat it up, and yet adults are astounded when I tell them this. They shouldn't be.

Based on this observation with younger audiences, as well as from having presented and performed thousands of silent film shows over the last forty years, I have come to believe that it is our right-brain function that makes silent film hold up. The mistake most people make is that they assume the left brain will be the roadblock.

There's no sound, no dialog. There's no color, aside from the monochrome range of "black and white." No data that one assumes would be necessary for the on-screen storytelling to work for the left brain. But it's precisely what's missing, what remains for our brain's right hemisphere to fill in and fuse together in our brain's cognitive yin-yang, that enables silent film to be as accessible a form of entertainment as "regular" film or video.

• • •

With silent film, we use our imagination to fill in the elements left out. As obvious as this may be to adults who have seen silent movies, it's ironic that there is an assumption that kids won't go for silents. Ironic, because children are in much better touch with and have better access to their imagination than grown-ups.

Parents and educators are always skeptical before screenings I've presented and accompanied—and so pleasantly surprised after—when their kids or students have attended. I can tell you—because I listen for it—that you can hear kids' laughter over the adults' at a show of a silent comedy film. Parents will tell me their youngster was almost doubled over laughing, and also admit they weren't expecting this.

The toys or dolls or anything children play with are small-scale representations of the real thing. No kid thinks "that's not a real car" or "that's a plastic scale model of a real person" or "those are just a bunch of small pieces of wood." If you get tagged in a game of "freeze tag," you aren't actually paralyzed, and touching the tree everyone's agreed is "base" doesn't actually make you immune to anything.

This play-based access to our imagination doesn't evaporate when we go through puberty or graduate from college. It is a condition of human thought that never leaves us, though it may be employed in different ways as we go through life. It is part of the human experience that we all possess, whether we are playing sports or games or are problem-solving or inventing.

This right-brain capacity isn't a human condition that only existed until 1929, when talking pictures changed the storytelling language of film and the way movies were made, both technologically and in performance.

• • •

Silent film has often been referred to as a universal language. It's true, but not just because the films are wordless, although that certainly levels the playing field. It's true because of that same leaving-out that is at the core of the medium's communication and storytelling.

There is something about silent film that tends to rely more on the universality of the human experience. By allowing us to assemble pieces of what we're seeing into gags, emotions, drama, and story, this same right-brain function we all possess kicks in, and in the same way.

The Cook (1918), starring and directed by Roscoe "Fatty" Arbuckle, with Buster Keaton and John Rand. Arbuckle's films have enjoyed a resurgence of interest and fandom in the past couple of decades.

Why else would a contemporary audience in South Korea get all the jokes and react with the same laughs as an American one for a 1920s silent comedy? I had an opportunity to accompany Keaton's *Steamboat Bill, Jr.* (1928) and Harold Lloyd's *The Freshman* (1925) at the Jecheon International Music and Film Festival in 2016 in South

Korea. The two shows were held outdoors, to audiences of close to 3,000 people. As "Roaring Twenties American" as one may think Harold Lloyd and the plot of *The Freshman* is, absolutely everything Lloyd and his gag writers put into the picture landed. I'd played for *Steamboat Bill, Jr.* a few times earlier that year, and—because I listen to the audience when I'm playing—I noticed that the audience in Jecheon not only laughed in the same places, but in the same way. The belly laughs, the smaller ones that built to a heartier second one, the laughs of surprise—they were all identical regardless of which audience I was experiencing during my shows.

The same goes for the audiences of sixth-graders in Tromsø, Norway, above the Arctic Circle, when I accompanied and helped to present Roscoe "Fatty" Arbuckle's *The Cook* (1918) and Buster Keaton's *One Week* (1920) as part of the annual Silent Film Days (Stumfilmdager) festival from 2006 to 2017. Ditto for the kindergartners I've shown the Stan Laurel comedy *Oranges and Lemons* (1923) to every year at a private school in New York City.

•   •   •

Silent film exists and is possible because of a fusing of core elements of the medium itself and our engagement. Silent film unwittingly engages us by the very absence of what talking pictures and, eventually, color brought to cinema. This melding of mind and moving picture happens almost instantly, as soon as the film begins. We are not aware of it happening. And yet, when the missing elements are considered in the abstract, the barrier most people have toward silent movies appears and is thought of as something that must be surmounted with some sort of mental concentration or effort.

This function of our brain's right hemisphere as part of this unique screen entertainment happens innately, unwittingly, instantaneously. It does so without conscious effort, the opposite of what is assumed by people who haven't experienced silent movies. The experience of watching a silent movie is, in some ways, like being in a sort of trance state, especially when it's in a theater and with live musical accompaniment.

The internationally renowned, Oscar-winning film historian and restorationist Kevin Brownlow references this essential and implicit facet of silent movies in the preface to his book *Hollywood: The Pioneers* (1979, Knopf). Brownlow writes of the involvement of the silent era's viewers: "They had to supply the voices and the sound effects, and because their minds were engaged, they appreciated the experience all the more. The audience was the final creative contributor to the process of making a film."

This is a point I make to audiences at my shows and is the basis of the course on silent cinema that I teach at Wesleyan University. It is as valid for today's viewers as it was over a hundred years ago.

• • •

The unique combination of the delivering of reality and the undepicted slivers of it that we process in that quasi dream state of experiencing silent film is what allows for an altered version of reality. There are several facets of what gets created in our minds. These happen through the leavings-out of pieces of story or character, the elision of elements of logic or consequence, and the occasional disregard of the laws of physics and gravity.

Oddly enough, our guide for navigating all of these are the people we see onscreen. As long as they are buying into what's going on, so will we. Story jumps, movements in time or space that are glossed over and shouldn't actually be possible, the existence of diegetic sound or the lack of it, and the weight of people and large objects—these are accepted by our onscreen playmates and, consequently, also by us.

Un Chien Andalou (1928), directed by Luis Buñuel and Salvador Dalí. Pierre Batcheff and Simone Mareuil are entranced by ants coming out of Pierre's palm.

This inadvertent unbridled license that allowed for the enhancement and reinvention of reality was used to even greater advantage by makers of serials and westerns and taken to the nth degree by comedians. It's no wonder the surrealists were fans of slapstick comedy shorts. There are countless silent era one- and two-reelers that possess dreamlike progressions of plot and action. The main difference between Luis Buñuel and Salvador Dalí's *Un Chien Andalou* (1928) and silent film comedies—think of Keaton's *The High Sign* (1921) or *The Goat* (1921)—is that the Dada payoffs to the setups in the Buñuel-Dali film are as far from the logical outcomes as possible.

•   •   •

I took a clown workshop several years ago and learned some basics of what clowning is—what the form and practice of being a clown *really* is. It's not just the red nose, makeup, oversized shoes, funny hats, or the hair and/or costuming that's had its edges amplified.

One of the main elements of clown, our teacher Eric Davis explained, is that it is something that happens with the audience. Literally, *with* the audience. Together. A key part of clown performance involves checking in with the people in the theater, making eye contact and connecting with them, reacting and sharing with them interpersonally. As a clown, you're interlocking with the audience, acknowledging together with them the experience that's being communicated and played with. Our teacher's analogy was that if you imagine two overlapping circles—one for the performer or clown, and one for the audience—where those two circles overlap is where clown happens.

With silent film, it is a very similar blend of communication. The only difference, interestingly, is that with silent film we the audience or viewer are interacting with an immutable form.

What all of this allows for, I believe, is the existence of what I am calling the Silent Film Universe. It inhabits an alternate plane of existence, one that is similar to the one we know from the realm outside of silent movies, but which is more plastic, elastic, and expressive. This universe evaporated in less than a year when synchronized sound and talking pictures arrived. This technology did not just add talk to cinema, it pulled the rug of play and poetry out from under it.

Silent film employs a variety of types of visual cues and prompts to invite us up into its stories. These techniques will be discussed in the following six chapters.

4.

SILENT FILM'S SOUNDSCAPE

One of my favorite natural laws of the Silent Film Universe involves, of all things, sound. That is, sound that happens in a scene, and whether or not it exists.

The acceptance of the sound that should be heard is selective, regardless of whether or not we see what or who is making that sound, and whether it ought to make a sound. In a stage production or a performance of a clown gag or piece of physical comedy business in a theater, there is a certain amount of room given the character's ability to hear something happening on stage or in a scene with them. The other person on stage may be tiptoeing around and trying not to make any noise. We will accept that the person they're hoping won't catch them doesn't hear them, so long as our primary character doesn't indicate they hear anything. Maybe.

In any motion picture form, we are presented with a real moving image of what is happening before the camera. Fact. In the Silent Film Universe, though, unless the character before the camera indicates they hear a sound that they ought to be hearing, that sound is not audible. It does not exist. Neither to the character in the film nor in our identification with their auditory experience—no matter how loud that sound is, and no matter how close the sound is to them.

Our interpretation of what sound exists or does not is interpreted for us by our onscreen guide, and we accept it.

One of my favorite examples of this is the closing gag in Keaton's *One Week* (1920). Buster and his new bride, played by Sybil Seely, are towing their recently assembled modular kit house across railroad tracks, and the house gets stuck. While Buster and Sybil are arguing about what to do next, there is a cut to a locomotive barreling down some nearby tracks, then to a close-up of the train whistle blowing, and then to Buster and his bride. They stop. They indicate to us that they have heard the whistle and train. They look down at the tracks they are standing on, then panic.

Summoning all their strength, they try to move the house out of the way, to no avail. Fortunately, the train diverts to another track—one we don't see, thanks to clever placement of the camera—and completely misses the house. Whew.

Buster and Sybil heave a sigh of relief. Cut to a big wide shot of the house, with Buster and Sybil between it and the camera. A second locomotive enters from frame right and plows through the house, demolishing it, surprising Buster, his bride, and us. It is one of the film's biggest laughs, and a stunning ending to one of the great comedy shorts of the silent era.

Why don't Buster and Sybil hear the second train?

Buster Keaton's *One Week* (1920), with Sybil Seely. That second train made just as much noise as the first one did.

It doesn't matter. That's the logic of the gag, and as long as they don't indicate that they have heard it, that other train does not make any sound. In fact, it does not exist to Buster and Sybil until it hits the house full-on, a half second after we see it enter the frame.

There are tons of examples of this law of selective audible sound in silent movies, in comedies and dramas and action pictures. Lions appear in a room our comedian is in, and may even snarl. But the comedian doesn't indicate that they have heard the lions right away, and may even take several seconds before they do and then react. Do we as an audience accept this? You bet.

In the Silent Film Universe, if a tree falls in the woods and the lumberjack does not indicate that they have heard it, it does not make a sound.

33

• • •

What did this absence or aberration of the presence of sound mean to people making silent film? While it is not known who figured this out or how or when it came into regular use, it was clearly a known entity of the world of silent movies. I'll bet that, if you weren't aware of it yourself, you may start noticing its use more now in films of the 1910s and 1920s.

It must have been liberating to have this element of nature be optional, that the existence of a sound could be selective per a character or characters in a scene in a film, and that it would be believable and accepted by the audience. In drama and comedy alike, it meant that a certain amount of logic and consequence could be dispensed with, in the interest of the expediency of keeping the story moving and gradually raising its stakes.

Imagine writing a scenario (the term for screenplays in the silent era) and having that much more possibility about what could happen next in a scene. An automobile in the same scene with your main characters, its noisy 1920s motor running, not noticed until the *ah-OOH-gah* of its Klaxon horn is heard...and then only by the director and editor selectively showing us a close-up of someone sounding it.

It must have been freeing to just think—okay, well, no one will hear that just yet, until the character "gets over" that they have heard it.[6]

---

[6] "Get over" is an expression I have seen in original silent movie scenarios that indicates that the performer physically reacts in some way that will tell viewers what that reaction is.

This is part of why I like to think of the world inhabited by silent film as its own universe. The natural laws of sound and whether or not they exist at a particular moment represent just one of the believable-by-us elisions of reality in the fantasy-of-fact—as Kerr refers to it—of silent movies.

•   •   •

There is another way that sound's existence, perceived by the onscreen character, can be bent.

A ventriloquist isn't actually throwing their voice, although that's often what the skill is called. The voice appears to be coming from the dummy because the ventriloquist is creating an illusion. She or he is paying attention to the dummy or puppet as if it were actually the one speaking. Similar misdirection can happen in silent film. Because of the medium's mute nature, a sound can happen in a different space or in a different way than it's registered as being heard—usually for comic effect.

Let's take the example of ripped pants in a couple different silent comedies. In the Stan Laurel solo short *Collars and Cuffs* (1923), there is a bit where Stan thinks he is repeatedly ripping his pants. We are shown what Stan is hearing: a woman who also works in the laundry where he is employed has a basket of shirt collars which she is tearing up, one by one. It's clear, from the way we are shown the space they are both in, that Stan and the woman, played by Katherine Grant, are maybe eight to ten feet away from each other.

In reality, you can hear the difference between a sound happening several feet away and a sound happening to the pants you are wearing. We should expect this of Stan, or of the young woman in the Laurel & Hardy comedy *The Finishing Touch* (1928), whom Stan and Ollie deliberately prank with this same device. The logic of this goes out the window. Because, as I've mentioned before, in the Silent Film Universe we believe what the performers onscreen believe.

In *The Navigator* (1924), Buster Keaton and Kathryn McGuire have been shanghaied on an empty ocean liner and are trying to make the best of things while waiting to be rescued. During one of their nights on the boat they huddle together in the ship's parlor, frightened. The boat's rocking causes a Victrola on the other side of the room to begin playing a record of "Asleep in the Deep." This record and the song were well known at the time, especially for the last line of the chorus, which is sung, usually by a male bass, in a very low register.

Buster and Kathryn *should* be able to tell that what they are hearing is a Victrola playing a record. The sound of that record with its male bass vocal solo is eerie, to be sure, but if you have heard a Victrola playing a shellac 78 rpm record, you know it doesn't sound exactly like someone in the room with you. It sounds like a record, and one with certain limitations on its tonal range. We actually don't know *what* it is Buster and Kathryn think they are hearing, but the context of the scene lets us know that it sounds ghostly and creepy to *them*.

In the climactic fight in Harold Lloyd's *The Kid Brother* (1927), the circus strongman—played by Constantine Romanoff—has cornered Lloyd in an abandoned ship. Lloyd is backed up against a wall, and Romanoff is wielding a piece of lead pipe. He hits Lloyd over the head with it. Nothing. He hits him again, and again…no reaction. This happens one more time. The strongman pauses, confused as to why the target of his blows is unharmed. Lloyd sees an opportunity and runs off, revealing a steel L brace on the wall that had been hidden by his head and hair. We realize that *this* is what Romanoff has been hitting with the lead pipe. Three times.

Harold Lloyd in *The Kid Brother* (1927), with Constantine Romanoff.
(courtesy of Harold Lloyd Entertainment)

At no point does the loud metallic *clank* that the two objects make when struck against each other tip him off. Both Romanoff and Lloyd play the purely visual reality of the gag, and the reveal of the object that has been hit gets a laugh. At no point do we think, "Wait a second…shouldn't the metallic clank have been obvious on the first hit?"

Besides, we're already onto the next beat of the fight and chase, absorbed in it. Lloyd and Romanoff don't stop to consider what has happened, and consequently neither do we.

Earlier in this chase sequence, there is a gag with a small monkey walking around the deck of the boat in human shoes, fooling the strongman into thinking it is Harold (who put his shoes on the monkey). As long as the strongman believes the rapid footsteps of a very small monkey are the same pace and volume as those of Mr. Lloyd, so do we.

Comedian Marcel Perez brilliantly makes use of this notion of perceived sound in his two-reeler *Lend Me Your Wife* (1916), which he also wrote and directed. A handful of people who have been chasing Perez around are in the living room of a house, and he has escaped them by climbing up the house to its roof. Perez gets an idea and goes over to the chimney and yells into it. A title card cuts in that says "Bo-oo-oo!" and then Perez cuts to the living room, where his adversaries hear this through the fireplace and are terrified. Perez is expecting us to imagine what the others hear, that his voice distorts and echoes when going from the top of a chimney all the way down the flue and out the fireplace into a room.

Articles promoting a silent movie show often use the phrase "silent movies were never really silent" when mentioning the live accompaniment. This is done to reassure readers that they won't be sitting in a library-like atmosphere during the screening. But the truth is that there is sound, all kinds of it, except that it exists in the viewer's imagination, as prompted by what happens on screen. The difference is that in the Silent Film Universe, the identity or existence of a sound need not be literal. This gave people making silent film a freedom of expression that was not tied to the literal reproduction of sound or to the expectation of reality that synchronized sound reinforces.

Having addressed the "silent" in silent film, we will now explore the different visual methods the medium utilizes to engage us in its storytelling.

5.

ICONOGRAPHY AND ARCHETYPES

Silent film engages us by telling us only a certain amount of detail about the story's players and events. Just enough that we can fill in the rest from our own knowledge and experiences in life. It's similar to the way these same kinds of story elements are presented in fairy tales and in books for young children.

What do we know about Little Red Riding Hood? Where does she buy the ingredients for the goodies she makes to take to her grandmother? And where are her parents? Cinderella has a wicked stepmother and two awful stepsisters, but we know nothing of her father and how the poor girl wound up in this situation.

How much backstory do we know about the Berenstain bears? Or Madeline? What do Christopher Robin's parents do for a living? Is the hero of *Mike Mulligan and His Steam Shovel* in a labor union, and does he have workers' comp?

Do we need any of this deep background info to go on the ride with the character and the story?

We are presented with archetypes in silent film, constantly, and it is left to us to fill in the rest. We are given hints in a character's costuming and physical demeanor.

Charlie Chaplin in *The Tramp* (1915).

A title will let us know someone is "the doctor from across the hall," "the local sheik," or "the town gossip." Sometimes we are told our protagonists are merely—as they are introduced to us in *Grandma's Boy* (1922)—"The Boy," "The Girl," "The Rival," and "His Old Fashioned Grandmother." This titular appellation is enough, and we go with it, filling in details (or not).

How Chaplin's little tramp came to be homeless is never mentioned. Nor what his name is. He is rarely identified in a title when introduced in a film. At the beginning of both *The Tramp* (1915) and *City Lights* (1931), he merely shows up in a rural town or a city somewhere, and it's left to us to identify who he is. The same goes for when we discover him in *Modern Times* (1936), industriously hard at work on an assembly line, for a change. As viewers we do not dwell on needing the backstory.

Similarly, we are not told how "The Woman from the City" in F. W. Murnau's *Sunrise* (1927) came to live in that small rural town or how it is that she and "The Man" have managed to have an affair that neither "The Wife" nor anyone else in the unnamed mythical hamlet of the story has caught on to. We are shown or told very simple, key details, the way they might be shown in a storybook, and nothing more. And yet, even though this is a movie in which we are watching people act out a narrative, having minimal detail does not cause question marks to appear over our heads about what is going on.

We absolutely would have questions, though, if it were a film with sync sound and color. In a sound film, our expectation of reality is much greater, and we therefore require more detail and personal background on our characters to meet this expectation and to justify what is going on. In the Silent Film Universe, our expectation of reality is lowered. Given a reduced amount of visual information, we generate the full reality by engaging our imagination.

This is another element of the Silent Film Universe that is not only unique to the medium, but that gave the creators of these films more room to keep the story moving and keep the stakes raised, as needed, without having to spend a ten- or eleven-minute reel setting up and justifying something.

• • •

When riding on a train, we know who the conductor is by their uniform. Seeing people wearing the same-colored polo shirt in a chain store tells us these people are employees there, and that they may (or may not) know where we can find what we are looking for. The type of apron worn by people working in a restaurant kitchen identifies which of them is responsible for the various food-prep roles and tasks. The storybook simplicity of the way we are fed information in silent film works the same way in its use of character archetypes.

In a silent movie, we don't have the capability to listen to a conversation in which a character mentions having been out on her yacht to figure out that she is wealthy. We also don't have the time for it. Sometimes an intertitle can give us that clue, but it's much easier and less of an interruption to show someone dressed a certain way and have just enough haughtiness in their physicality for us to figure out who they are.

The use of character archetypes is a visual shorthand for viewers, so we know who everybody is, instantly, when we see them. This way, we can get right on to the business or story point or gag setup and keep things moving along. We pick up these clues, even from people who are not wearing uniforms. Granted, one may need a certain amount of knowledge of the culture of the time when watching a movie from the 1910s or 1920s—such as knowing about "floorwalkers" in a department store—but the costuming iconography is still there to indicate quickly who's who.

It's like opening your front door on Halloween and seeing a bunch of kids in different costumes. You know who's dressed as what. (Well, most of the time.)

I'm not exactly sure how or when this became part of the silent film storytelling lexicon. It obviously comes from stage traditions, but what's interesting is that the practice takes hold as a visual shorthand early on, in early-1910s cinema, and is maintained throughout the rest of the silent era. It doesn't completely disappear when sound comes in, of course, but it is no longer used as a key identifier of who someone is or what their occupation or background or class is, because we now have dialog and conversation to inform us.

With silent film, we're shown a big hint, and even without a lot of detail we take the hint and that's usually enough. The balance of how much is or isn't given to us is part of the medium's cinematic language.

•   •   •

The visual shorthand employed in silent film helps us know immediately what sort of behavior to expect of the person we see on screen. It invites us to make assumptions about their needs or wants or fears, and assumes we all have a shared expectation of a character who has a certain look or way of moving or dressing. This is where our right brain dovetails with silent film's storytelling shorthand.

We know that when a mustachioed man driving a wagon full of dogs and carrying a large net shows up in any Our Gang comedy, the kids had better hide their dog Pete. Erich von Stroheim, in his uniform, monocle, and sly sneer, will undoubtedly be some sort of threat to our leading lady, whether it's in *Foolish Wives* (1922) or *The Wedding March* (1928).

It's not just stage traditions or Halloween or children's dress-up games that rely on this type of identification. It's part of many social interactions. Uniforms of different types continue to signify identities, even today when an effort is being made by many to move away from the stereotyping or "profiling" of "you look like ____ so I expect that you are/will ____."

The ethnic stereotyping we see in silent movies is a cultural artifact of its time, but is not part of the language of silent film itself. It's a component of the way the language was used in the 1910s and 1920s, especially in comedies. It was part of a set of shared expectations or behavioral assumptions that was—for better or worse—common or rampant at the time.

In *Bumping into Broadway* (1919), Harold Lloyd hides from his burly landlady by diving into a large basket of laundry. Moments later, two Asian-presenting men (played by Caucasians) wearing attire audiences were expected to recognize as being Chinese come to collect the basket. The men lift the basket and the bottom gives way, revealing Lloyd to his landlady, and the chase resumes. The racist aspect of the gag counted on the audience's assumption that the two Chinese men are laundry workers, which would explain why they have entered the scene and prompt the audience to anticipate the peril Harold is about to be in. There are many fright gags in silent comedies involving

African Americans who, it appears, were assumed to be extremely frightened by just about anything.[7]

These stereotype-driven usages are often uncomfortable to view through today's eyes and mindsets, and will continue to be. But at the time these films were made, this was part of the known cultural lexicon and was used occasionally in silent movies as part of the storytelling shorthand.

This particular usage is specific to movies made during the silent era, but is not essential to silent film language.

• • •

The visual shorthand of silent film also functions with physical objects. Often, by connecting them with other objects or between shots of people, an impression is intended to be made on viewers, rather than blatantly spelling out the point.

The iconography of the items or what they represent may be all that we are given, and all we need. Makers of silent film had been using this in different ways since the 1910s, but the technique develops into an art form of suggestion in the early or mid-1920s.

In *He Who Gets Slapped* (1924), directed by Victor Seastrom, there is a moment toward the end when the romantic relationship of two of the main characters, played by Marc McDermott and Ruth King, takes a turn. The scene fades in and we are in a room in the woman's home, one we have seen before. What we are shown is, simply:

---

[7] I have noticed that these scare gag sequences appear primarily in comedy films made in 1924–1925; there is history to be researched that may help to explain this.

- a close medium shot of King sitting in a chair—she sees someone offscreen, then her face and eyes follow something moving downward

- a close-up of a chair, on which we see a top hat, gloves, and a cane—a man's hand enters the shot and picks up the gloves, then the hat, then the cane

- King watching this happen, distraught

- a medium wide shot of the doorway out of the room—McDermott enters the shot on his way out of the room, briefly looks back, and exits, pulling the door shut

- King, taking this in slowly, then looking down

- a close-up of a check made out to her for thousands of francs; the number followed by zeroes is covered by her thumb

There is no title in the sequence. We do not see the man enter the room, nor what happened between the two before the scene begins. The man and the woman do not speak to one another. The actions I have described above merely happen.

And yet, we know exactly what has occurred. It may not be clear from my description, if you don't know the film, but from the story context, and what the objects mean in societal conventions (of the time), it's clear that the relationship is over. Even viewed now during a time when making sure you left a place with your hat has been extinct for decades, being shown only suggestions of actions and reactions, we can not only deduce what each of the shots symbolizes but also fuse this all together into a narrative moment.

We are told or shown very little...and we understand everything.

Marc McDermott, Tully Marshall, and Norma Shearer in a scene from *He Who Gets Slapped* (1924). (courtesy of Jon C. Mirsalis)

6.

SILENT FILM LEAVES IT OUT,
WE FILL IT IN

The Silent Film Universe invites us into it by deliberately *not* providing important visual information in a sequence of moments. Key information about action in a scene and insight into a character's thoughts is presented to us by leaving these details out, instead giving us visual cues that either bookend the information or serve as a chain of hints whose connection to one another is not delineated.

On the surface, this doesn't seem logical. After all, if you ordered a bacon-lettuce-tomato sandwich at a deli or restaurant and it was served without the bacon, lettuce, or tomato, you'd send that BLT back. This is, precisely, the way silent film delivers the sandwich—yet when we take a bite, it is exactly what we ordered. Our imagination fills in the missing ingredients, drawing on our understanding and experiences of life and its emotions.

Silent film's visual shorthand can also ask us to conjure up an event or physical act by not showing it at all. Films in the 1930s, or earlier, might avoid depicting something particularly nasty by cutting to a shot showing the shadows of the actors on a wall. Silent film, because of its absence of recorded sync sound, has the ability to skip the visual euphemism and remove any depiction of an action.

In an early scene in *The Mark of Zorro* (1920) with Douglas Fairbanks, Zorro is almost literally conjured up by big bad Sergeant Gonzales (Noah Beery) and some men in a pub. All you have to do to make Zorro appear, one of his men tells the Sergeant via a title card, is to harm one of the "natives." We are then shown

- Gonzales reacting to this information—he gets an idea

- a group of Indigenous locals across the room, cowering in fear

- Gonzales, who moves toward them

- Gonzales's men, aghast at something intense that occurs offscreen

- one of the locals, fallen to the floor, with Gonzales standing over him and holding his sword

Not only is the act of violence not shown, it is one that ought to involve some loud and anguished sounds. The act takes place in less time than it would have realistically, had it actually been shown, even if it had been elided in screen time through edits. Gonzales's men do not "get over" that they are seeing an assault or hearing the victim cry out.

Douglas Fairbanks in *The Mark of Zorro* (1920), with Noah Beery, Sr.
(courtesy of Robert Arkus)

But we know exactly what has happened. When I show this film to my university students in our class session on Fairbanks, they have no trouble understanding what has happened, even without the benefit of exposure to the ten or fifteen years of silent film storytelling that audiences of 1920 would have experienced.

There is a similar moment in Josef von Sternberg's *The Docks of New York* (1928). Toward the end of the film, there is a contentious scene between Mae (Betty Compson) and Andy (Mitchell Lewis). Andy is an engineer on the steamer that he and the film's main character, Bill Roberts (George Bancroft), are on shore leave from. Andy seems to be advancing on Mae, seemingly pressuring or maybe threatening her. It's not delineated to us, specifically. We cut to a doorway, and Andy's wife (Olga Baclanova), with her back to us, slowly enters the room, closing the door behind her.

Cut to a window inside the room. There are seagulls at the window. After a second or two the seagulls fly away. Cut to Roberts in a nearby café; he looks up, reacting to something. His reaction is not one of panic or surprise, just enough to get over that something outside has happened that he has noticed. There is a commotion outside—people are running about, and they and the police rush upstairs to the apartment. What follows, visually, does not spell out for us clearly what has just happened. There is not a medium shot of Andy's wife or Mae holding a smoldering pistol, nodding in smug satisfaction, or of Andy clutching a wound, falling to the ground.

It is not for another thirty seconds of screen time that it becomes clear to us that Andy has been murdered. It is left to us to figure all this out during the few shots that *follow,* by which time we are almost too caught up in the flow of the excitement to go back and realize, "Oh, *that's* why we saw the seagulls and why they suddenly flew away."

Three more minutes of screen time pass before we are informed that it is Andy's wife who shot him.

It's possible that, watching this film, you might wonder about the visual near-non-sequitur of a shot of a window with seagulls in it. Their flying away is in reaction to the loud gunshot. But this is not spelled out for us. Not even in a hint. We are asked by von Sternberg to infer just from the tension in the room that the reason the birds suddenly fly away is that something has startled them. We don't find out that a gun has been fired until later.

I have often wondered about this sequence and how it might have been understood by 1928 audiences. Did a drummer in the orchestra pit hit a rim shot? Did a pianist smack a cluster of keys? Or, more probably, was the accompaniment just continuing along with the "agitato" music undoubtedly indicated in the score's cue sheet?[8]

Since scoring was done in the theaters by the local musicians, either making their own choices or following the issued cue sheet, it was probably a range of these options.

This moment is one I am still working on as far as how I underscore and support it. When I've played for the film, I've leaned toward something in the middle, building tension toward a panic chord—but not a sound effect key slam—that coincides with the birds taking off, in case a contemporary audience might not have been able to synthesize all this. Sometimes you are supporting the audience as well as the film.

These sequences from *Zorro* and *Docks* point to the poetry of silent film and its reliance on the viewer's imagination and right-brain experience to tell a story.

• • •

Soviet cinema of the 1920s takes silent film's technique of showing us something that represents a fuller picture—for us to fill out—to another level. Filmmakers like Pudovkin, Eisenstein, Vertov, and others, borrowing

[8] During the silent film era, musical accompaniment was often guided by "cue sheets," playlists of stock "mood" music that indicated a piece for a given scene.

some of the editing techniques seen in D. W. Griffith's films to build tension or create an impression, used this visual technique to have the viewer fuse a few elements instead of just giving the audience a single hint to expand on.

They were often deliberately making a point, and so the single hint may not have been enough.

They built on what Griffith had pulled off with his film *Intolerance* (1916), particularly during its final half hour. The crosscutting and building of tension to a dramatic climax that is paralleled across four different stories from four different eras was an example of how you could mash up a number of disparate elements to make one overall point. As off-putting as the running time, scale, and multi-epochal narrative of *Intolerance* may seem, I can tell you that—at least at shows of this film that I have accompanied—once that buildup gets going, the cutting back and forth between the four stories' chases and battles in the final minutes of the film is really exciting for an audience.

Soviet filmmakers combined this with the "we're only going to show you this much" suggestive technique by cutting from one suggested object, person, or symbol to another, and then another, and then another. Instead of the impression being built up over the course of an entire reel of film, it happens within a few or several seconds.

This technique can also be used, over and over, building gradually throughout a sequence, as it is in the battle on the Odessa steps in Eisenstein's *Battleship Potemkin* (1925) or the "spring thaw" protest and chase at the end of Pudovkin's film *Mother* (1926).

In *Potemkin*, Eisenstein combines angled wide shots of soldiers descending the steps with medium shots and close-ups of a mother clutching her son while advancing upward toward the soldiers. Both perspectives are shown in both static and moving-camera shots. Rather than show both elements in a single wide shot or shots, we are invited to combine the images of the soldiers with those of the mother and child as they move in opposite screen directions.

Pudovkin's *Mother* is the story of Pavel, a young factory worker who lives with his parents and is involved with the proletarian movement. Toward the end of the film, he has been imprisoned after leaflets and weapons he has hidden under the floorboards are found by authorities. Pavel's mother tries to help him, and eventually his comrades plan a prison break. The tension builds as the prisoners are marched through the prison yard, while a crowd of protesters gather outside and head toward the jail.

In the frenzied closing minutes of *Mother*, Pudovkin presents us with this sequence of shots:

- close-up of the bell of a bugle being blown, pointed straight at the camera

- title: "Across the bridge to the prison!"

- low-angle frontal wide shot of the bridge, which is empty

- medium wide shot of large blocks of snow-covered ice flowing laterally right to left in a river

- three short closer shots of ice blocks in the river breaking against the riverbed

- frontal wide shot of ice flowing in a river, moving toward the camera

- overhead wide shot of large crowd of protesters, seen from the back, walking toward the bridge

- medium close-up, from the opposite side of the crowd, showing Pavel's mother marching with the group

- overhead wide shot of protesters; a flag is passed from the back of the group to the front

- close-up of Pavel's mother

- close-up of flag, held aloft and rippling in the wind

- head-and-shoulders shot of the man holding the pole of the flag

- the flag

- the man holding the pole, but a lower shot that only shows his torso, emphasizing his hands holding the pole

- ice flowing in the river toward the camera

- closer shot of ice flowing; a large block of it moves past the camera

- low-angle wide shot of the bridge

- overhead wide shot of the prison yard, where the prison break is about to take place

All of this takes place during approximately one minute of screen time. We are simply shown these visual components without explanation of why we are being shown them or the reason for their sequence. It is up to us to assemble these in our minds.

This silent film technique works on a similar principle to the one where only a suggestion of a dramatic element is shown. The difference here is that we in the audience use our engaged right brain to come up with the rest from, in its shortest and simplest manifestation, three items—the first thing we are shown, the second, and the cut between the two. The sequence from *Mother* does this in a longer chain of visual elements that we fuse together.

If I mention an orange with cloves stuck in it, it will conjure up stories or memories for you, fully illustrated. What Soviet montage did is more like blending ingredients in a mixing bowl, or making your morning coffee just the way you like it.

• • •

The same practice is utilized to bring us inside the minds of the characters on screen. The simplest form of this is the basic equation of showing someone looking at something, showing us what they are seeing, and then showing that person reacting to or thinking over what they have seen. It can also be expanded to invite us to use our life experiences to think of what the onscreen character is considering.

The end of Chaplin's *City Lights* (1931) is one of the greatest examples of this. When the blind woman, now seeing, puts the coin into Charlie's hand and recognizes him by feel, Chaplin the director holds on a close-up of the Blind Girl's face. She is remembering everything that has happened over the film's previous eighty or more minutes. So are we. When the camera moves to Charlie's face, we see and understand that *he* is remembering the same thing. So are we. We are also empathizing first with the Blind Girl's emotional reaction, and then with Charlie's. No title cards, no gestures reminding each other of the past events, no flashback montage. And yet we know exactly what these two are thinking…and feeling.

When Blake Edwards's movie musical *Victor/Victoria* (1985) was adapted into a Broadway show, one big part of the characters' stories could not be carried over from screen to stage. This was the running gag of cutting to close-ups of different characters in the story thinking, "Wait a second, is that person actually…?"—which is half of the overall concept of the film.

This cinematic ability to allow the viewer to know the thoughts of a character is a facet of cinema that silent film utilizes even more freely and more frequently than sound film does.

The use of reaction shots in silent film does not need to be limited to a main character, or to just one or two characters as might be the case in a Laurel & Hardy film.

With Stan and Ollie, when we watch and take in their mental states, it's done with purpose. Ollie looks into the camera, asking us for sympathy; Stan looks into the camera not so much to communicate with us as to allow us a window into the slowly turning cogs in his mind. It's the same with comedian Harry Langdon, whose reactions lasted even longer than Laurel's, whether he was reacting to a cyclone hitting town or his own sneezes.

With silent film, however, this is still possible without characters breaking the fourth wall. It can happen with as many characters as the filmmakers wish. Dramatic action and beats can happen without a character's being in conversation or interaction with another. A mark of a great screen performer is their gift for expressing to us what the characters they are portraying are thinking without obvious eyebrow raises or anything deliberate like that.

Mary MacLaren in *Shoes* (1916), directed by Lois Weber.
(courtesy of Eye Filmmuseum)

There is a moment in *The New York Hat* (1912) when Mary Pickford thinks about and pines for the fancy hat we have seen her observe longingly in a shop window. It's practically a monologue or soliloquy, purely of thought, which we can follow. The lead character in Lois Weber's *Shoes* (1916), played by Mary MacLaren, has a similar moment late in the film. Without hints in titles or anything else, we watch her—in sustained long takes—consider her circumstances and make the decision that she has been grappling with for the entire duration of the film.

In both cases, we are invited into the character's internal monologue or thought process. And we bring something of our shared human experience to what we are seeing in order to decode and empathize with the character onscreen.

This is possible with two characters interacting in the same scene, as well as with isolated close-ups of those characters. The sequence from *He Who Gets Slapped* (1924) mentioned earlier—in which a couple ends their relationship—works because, in addition to knowing what the simple actions shown represent, we are also providing for ourselves the *thoughts* of both characters, even though neither says anything to each other.

• • •

The opening sequence of Pudovkin's *Mother* functions the same way, but with three perspectives—the laborer husband, the wife he comes home to, and their son Pavel.

The husband enters the home, slightly drunk, preceded by an intertitle that says, "The Father." His wife looks up at him. He looks at the wind-up clock on the wall and at the iron hanging from it as a weight. We see Pavel in a bed, asleep. There is then a sequence of close shots of the father and the mother, watching each other, as the father goes to the clock, unhooks the iron, and pockets it. The mother goes to him and grabs him—he falls, the noise waking Pavel. The father advances on the mother, raising his arm to retaliate. Pavel gets out of bed and defends his mother, stopping the attack.

Pudovkin covers this almost exclusively in close-up or close medium shots of the father, the mother, and Pavel—looking at each other, understanding what the other is doing, and reacting—and inserts of the iron, a clenched fist, and a hammer Pavel grabs off the floor. It isn't until a few reaction shots between Pavel and his father that we are given an intertitle, in which Pavel tells his father to leave his mother alone. There isn't another title in the rest of the scene, the entirety of which takes up nearly two minutes of screen time.

Aside from this one line, none of the three of them speak to each other during the sequence. Not only are we providing their thoughts for ourselves, but there are also two things the sequence gets away with only because of the latitude of expression allowed in the medium of silent film. We accept the interaction and conflict even though in real life these three people would have said things, angrily and passionately, to each other. Additionally, the reason the husband takes the iron is only divulged—without titles or any other deliberate explanation—by our being shown the *next* scene...when the husband enters a pub and tries to pay the bartender for a drink with the iron. Oh...*that's* what he was planning and thinking when he got home in the previous scene.

• • •

One of my favorite examples of how far this technique can be taken is evidenced throughout *Lady Windermere's Fan* (1925), directed by Ernst Lubitsch. All the characters in the film are constantly trying to figure out what the others in the scene with them are up to, or are reacting to something the other has done and trying to figure out why. Sometimes the titles clue us in, but mostly it's left to us viewers to enter the mind or mindset of the character, and then that of the next person when we cut to them, and then the next. A good deal of the film's dramatic action and storyline is told entirely through reaction shots—reaction shots which, in a sound film or a stage play, would have included the character responding verbally in some way.

Silent film allows for characters to have reactions that are entirely nonverbal, and we accept these reactions without any dialog and learn through them what each character is thinking or considering.

7.

SILENT FILM'S USE OF TEXT

If there is one other ubiquitous stereotype people have about silent movies besides heightened or exaggerated gesturing, it is the use of title cards—and rightfully so. Intertitles *are* a genuine component of silent cinema's visual means of imparting information to the viewer, and they serve a variety of functions. They are also part of the engaged experience we have with silent film.

The title cards bearing text that appear in silent film were originally referred to as sub-titles, rather than intertitles. Since the term "subtitles" today more commonly describes text superimposed over the bottom of an image, for the purposes of this book, I will refer to the title cards in silent film as "intertitles."

These first appeared in motion pictures made in the first decade of the 1900s, and were placed in films to separate scenes, often serving to announce not only the scene change but also precisely what we were about to see happen in the scene that followed. In *The Evidence of the Film* (1913), made by the Thanhouser Company, we are presented with a title that reads: "The dishonest broker plots to outwit his client." This is followed by a long, sustained take in medium wide shot, in the broker's office, during which we see exactly what was described played out by the characters in the scene. In the Griffith-directed Biograph short *The Lonedale Operator* (1911), a title informs us: "Her father ill, she takes his place at the key." The shot that follows shows us the woman's elderly father clearly unwell. The woman comforts him and assures him— pointing to the door and then to herself while talking— that he should go home and she will take care of sending and receiving telegraphed messages.

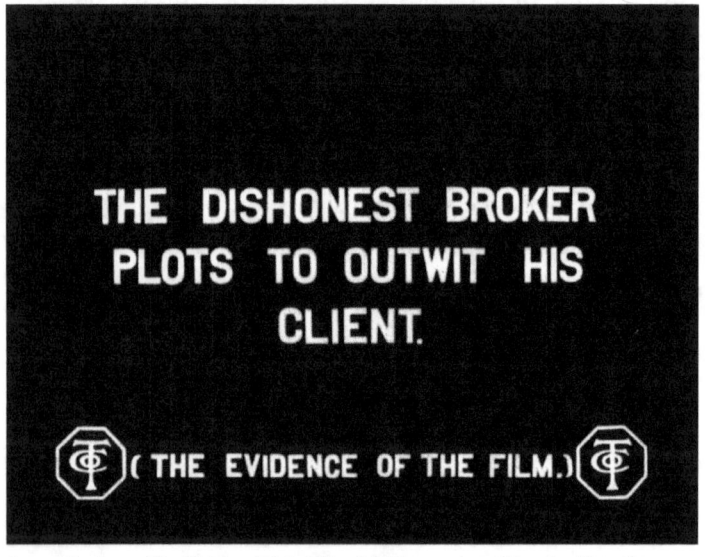

Intertitle from *The Evidence of the Film* (1913), produced by the Thanhouser Film Corporation. (courtesy of Library of Congress)

This may seem like overkill to us today, but these titles may have helped the working-class audiences of the time, many of whom were still learning English, to comprehend the scene that followed. Although today we would expect the word "SPOILER" to appear at the top of these, they served to give the audience enough information without having to frequently interrupt the action to explain who everybody was, what they were doing, and why. The way you would when watching a movie with a small child.

These titles, like all silent film intertitles, bring us information…and just enough of it. These "announcement"-type titles that introduced a scene gradually gave way during the mid-1910s to ones that did not blatantly divulge the proceedings that would follow. Additionally, a title might occasionally appear within a scene to give another hint every once in a while, just enough so no one would be lost. The viewer was now being trusted more to inherently understand what was being shown.

The use of intertitles in silent film became an art unto itself, in terms of the craft of the wording, the economy of the word count, and the amount of information being leaked to us. There were developments in the use of existing typefaces and the creation of new ones. The use of art drawings, superimposed images, and textured backgrounds made their way into titling. These were not there just to be fancy, but there were aesthetic reasons for these developments as well as the insertion of titles when they may not really have been necessary.

The line spacing, type size, and margins also appear to have been standardized, either deliberately or through practice and trial and error. These typographical practices improved the readability of the intertitles, so that audiences could get the information they needed with only a brief interruption of the film—just enough to know what was what, while still filling in specifics with their own imagination.

• • •

One type of intertitle in silent film is the expository intertitle. A disembodied narrator we never meet, who, appears only sparingly, gives us just enough information to know where we are, or when, or that there has been a shift in dramatic action.

In silent film, an expository intertitle is the first thing we are shown following the film's main title. In some cases, it might be multiple intertitles, as in the ones that establish the historical setting of the French Revolution in D. W. Griffith's *Orphans of the Storm* (1921). Charlie Chaplin's *A Dog's Life* (1918), by contrast, opens with a single title card with nothing more than the word "Dawn."

Sometimes an expository title's purpose is nothing more than to let us know it is the following day. Sometimes we learn that it is now ten years later, or that Johnny is now an adult, or that someone's uncle has passed away and left them a fortune. The location may have changed, and just in case we have never seen or been to Death Valley or Niagara Falls, the title card tells us that that is where we are. There may be a passage of time between locations, or a jump in time and space during an action sequence. The latter is evidenced in the intertitle that says, "Seven floors higher," which appears in the middle of a chase up and down flights of stairs in an apartment building in Keaton's *The Goat* (1921).

Who is this narrator? We don't know. We are never introduced to them. This external voice of the story just exists, and drops in from time to time, as needed. It does not appear with a consistency or regularity during a film. The external narrator sets us off on our journey at the beginning of the film, but regardless of whether we count on our storyteller guide to be there or not, they do not always return at the end to wrap the story up. That "Once upon a time" title card at the outset of a silent film is there to get us situated. Like a server in a restaurant, it shows us to our table and lets us know the specials, but when the meal is over and the check is paid, we can find our coats and make our way out of the café on our own.

Intertitle from rom *One a Minute* (1920) starring Douglas MacLean and produced by Thomas H. Ince. The Ince studios were at the forefront of the use of "art titles". Using drawings or textured backgrounds creates a visually smoother transition than a plain black background.
(courtesy of Library of Congress)

The expository intertitle is one of the types of title cards we expect in silent film and immediately accept, even if we have never seen a silent film before. In my many years of accompanying or presenting silents and doing Q and A's, no one has ever asked who that disembodied narrator was supposed to be, and why they gradually disappear over the course of the film.

There are exceptions, of course, when the main character is our narrator and the titles are therefore set in the first person. John Ford's *Kentucky Pride* (1925) takes this a step further—the intertitle teller of the tale in the film is a horse. (Yes, you read that right.)

As members of the audience of a silent film, we take in the information shared, and as soon as we are out of the title and into the next shot, we are already fusing it with what we are seeing to make the story happen. It's like being at a wedding reception and having a cousin lean over, point at a woman farther down the buffet line, and tell you, *sotto voce,* "That's his uncle's ex-wife." Just enough information so you don't get lost, and can follow the proceedings.

• • •

The Silent Film Universe allows for us to shift from the perspective of one character to another very easily. In fact, with silent film, this is not something we are aware of as an audience. It is a natural part of the narrative landscape and does not come off as a clever device. It is something that may be possible in sound film or in literature, but is usually explained to us, and in sound film is used to demonstrate multiple viewpoints of the same story.

In films like *Citizen Kane* (1941) or *Rashomon* (1950), we are presented with multiple versions of a particular story, some of which overlap, as seen through the perspective or memory of a number of characters in the narrative. It is made clear that we are going from one person's perspective or memory-tale to another. We go from the story's present to that character's story, then back, then on to another's, and so forth, usually through the smooth transition of a dissolve. Not only are we aware it is being done, but this type of narrative device is also what these two films are known for.

The silent comedy one-reeler *Not Guilty* (1926), directed by Harry Sweet and starring Charles Puffy, uses this same concept, with the springboard of court testimony to move in and out of the refracted memories. So does René Clair's hilarious silent feature *Les Deux Timides* (1928), although it does so only during its courtroom sequence at the beginning.

Silent film, however, had been using this perspective shifting since the 1910s, although not as a device to show us different versions of the same tale. It did so without clueing the audience in to it, and without going in and out from the main perspective of a character in the story. It did this through a creative use of intertitles.

You may not even have been aware this was happening. It is done often enough that if you have seen several silent movies, or more, the technique just blends in unconsciously as part of the storytelling. It is silent film's dreamlike, looser grip on reality—or its offering of a different reality—that allows for that kind of storytelling freedom. Our right-brain function, or the yin-yang of the left-right hemisphere interaction, allows for this.

There are title cards that present us with exposition, with dialog internal to the scene, or with statements about a character's thoughts that put us inside their mind. Some of these titles may identify an object a character is looking at, which could be from either the objective narration or the internal thoughts of the character...or both.

In the 1916 short *Local Showers*, from the "Mishaps of Musty Suffer" comedy serial, Musty (Harry Watson, Jr.) is plagued with an aching tooth. When we are introduced to Mr. Suffer and his swollen cheek, a title announces, "The morning zephyrs set Musty's hollow tooth a-going," and then, "So off to the painless dentist goes Musty." When Musty encounters the receptionist, a title informs us, "She just can't bear the thought of what's going to happen to our hero," allowing us to understand why she looks so sad. After Musty has been sitting in the waiting room, the dentist's assistant puts on earmuffs and we are shown a title that reads, "I'm so tender-hearted I can't stand to hear 'em howl." The assistant is not addressing Musty, nor is he looking into the camera—we are now privy to his inner monologue. The film's next three intertitles are dialog spoken by one character to another, text identifying the dentist, and one that says "Local showers" as a wry comment on Musty being doused with water to revive him after his tooth has been pulled.

What makes this multi-perspective shifting practice unique to silent film is that these just happen via a cut, and *we* smoothly make the shift from one perspective to another, without being aware it is happening. With silent film there can be multiple perspectives to the story's narrative, given to us through text inserted before or during the live-action scenes we are watching.

• • •

Sometimes the expository intertitles in silent film may have a little more personality or a persona to them, but not always consistently throughout the picture. This is not set up for us in any way—it merely happens.

One somewhat prominent example of this is the late-1910s and early-1920s feature-length films of D. W. Griffith. A point is made about the idea of intolerance throughout the 1916 movie of the same name. Griffith does not identify himself as the speaker, but his presence is known enough that we know who it is. The film also has expository titles pointing out to us that people in society's upper echelons have no empathy for the poor and the downtrodden, without stating explicitly that it is Griffith himself speaking to us. The same is true of *Orphans of the Storm* (1921). There are multi-sentenced title cards that let us know that time has passed, what has happened to Lillian and Dorothy Gish's characters, and so forth. But there are other cards with similarly lengthy word counts that speak dismissively of aristocrats' "pussy-footing" behavior.

What is unique about this kind of usage is that as viewers we accept it and are not completely thrown by the fact that the director/auteur's mindset has bled over into the narration—and we don't wonder where it went in the next five or six of the film's expository titles.

Chaplin does something similar, although with a much smaller word count. *The Immigrant* (1917) has titles that read, simply, "Edna and her mother," "Alone and hungry," or the dialog title "'He was ten cents short.'" Chaplin's own viewpoint leaks into intertitles with light sarcasm in other places. When the boat of immigrants approaches Ellis Island, there is a title card that reads, "Arrival in the land of liberty." The immigrants gaze in awe at the Statue of Liberty and then, moments later, are roped off like cattle by the ship's officers. In Chaplin's *Behind the Screen* (1916), the title "The comedy department trying something new" is followed by a pie fight (which was already passé in 1916).

Intertitle from the Snub Pollard comedy *Do Me a Favor* (1923), produced by Hal Roach Studios. (courtesy of Library of Congress)

In these two cases, the point is made in the shot(s) after the title has appeared. The difference here is that the point is not made onscreen—it gets made in our mind. *We* assemble the title and the action. Chaplin has made his ironic point: "liberty" vs. being roped in, or "something new" with custard pies, which by 1916 were an unwelcome and worn-out comedy trope.

There were title writers who definitely brought a little more personality to their text, usually in comedies. Many of Douglas Fairbanks's 1915–1920 pre-Zorro "coat-and-tie" films have a sense of whimsy and fun in their intertitles, which were written by Anita Loos. The style neatly meets the fun Doug is clearly having outside of the titles.

You can tell the handiwork of H. M. "Beanie" Walker's title writing in Snub Pollard, Charley Chase, or Laurel & Hardy comedies, even if you have dipped in to a mid-1920s short in the middle without knowing it is a Hal Roach–produced comedy.

There is room within the form or format of expository intertitles in silent film for more than one perspective, and our human imagination will buy it, because we are in the state of narrative flow that only exists in the experience of silent film.

• • •

There is a conciseness to the text in the intertitles in silent film. Even in the wordy expository titles, there is a care and often a precision and an economy taken in expressing what needs to be gotten across in a sentence, or two. After all, the title card is something of an interruption, one that needs to be easy to read, since we would like to get back to the action.

It is a kind of writing whose expressiveness and brevity lies somewhere between writing prose and writing haiku. Dialog titles are the same, with just enough words to let us know what we need to know—just enough—to follow what's going on. They don't spell *everything* out, or go into great detail, or precisely transcribe dialog being spoken onscreen—they just convey the minimal amount of detail we need so we don't get lost.

The insertion of an intertitle also unwittingly asks us to access our imagination. It fills in a bit about what we have been watching, just at the moment before we may begin to wonder "who is *that*?" or "what's *she* doing here?" It may also occur in the moment that just precedes something that could be thought of as coming out of left field.

Sometimes it's both.

We synthesize the intertitle card with what has just preceded it and/or with what follows.

With dialog titles, it is more of a linear or literal use, of course. But with dialog we are just getting the distillation of what might be said in reality, and at that only a piece of the whole conversation. "Hand me that apron." "My husband!" "Bathe the Duke." "Zorro!"

Often, a few sentences have passed between the two people in the scene, but we only are given one of them. Sometimes the line of dialog has been boiled down to a handful of words. Just enough to get across the important point of the conversation that we can't infer from faces and subdued gestures. Just enough to fill in what we might not be able to ascertain or decode from the live action we are watching, whether it is dialog or exposition or the mentioning of a detail.

Did anyone plan this out, think it through, sit around smoking a pipe and scratching their chin in 1910 at a salon regularly visited by post–nickelodeon era moving picture directors? I doubt it. And yet, the economic style of intertitle writing in silent film and the usages of title insertions are pretty consistent from a point in the early-to-mid-1910s through the end of the silent era.

• • •

Intertitles in silent film also serve the function, mentally, of taking a cleansing breath. They provide a brief pause for our imagination from all the live-action storytelling we have been processing.

You may wonder how necessary all those titles are in silent film. Some of them may be full of poetic language or may look like the title writer was paid by the word. (Some of them were.) Some of them may just say "Later" or "The next day," something we could probably figure out from whatever we take in during the next shot we see.

I have watched many silent films whose intertitles do not survive at all or only survive as a frame or two (known as "flash titles"), and I can tell you that doing so is exhausting. With all the visual stimuli we are constantly ingesting and assembling in our brains, every once in a while, you need that break—for your brain to figuratively inhale and exhale.

Those titles serve a purpose. They are a page turn at the end of a chapter. A pause to refresh. Not a big break, like a seventh-inning stretch, but just a little semicolon to separate one scene from another—the way the mouth wiper in the feeding-machine sequence of Chaplin's *Modern Times* (1936) politely separates each of the dishes the device forces on assembly-line worker Charlie.

8.

PERFORMANCE TECHNIQUES
IN SILENT FILM

In silent cinema, performers convey information and emotion to us in their movement, gestures, and expressions. They have to. The movement styles and techniques we see in silent film range from obvious gesturing—what some assume is typical of pre-1930s movies—to profoundly underplayed emotional stillness. Some of that gesturing is so outdated it is hard for a contemporary audience to decipher.

A majority of performers in silent movies came from the theater, and one major technique they knew and had used in their craft was a catalog of gestures and expressions outlined by François Delsarte (1811–1871). Delsarte developed a "System of Expression" that was in essence a cataloguing of gestures and body language used in acting and performance. These gestures, or "attitudes," as they were referred to at the time, range from movements of the whole body to positionings of limbs, hands, and the head, down to minute movements of fingers, eyes, and eyebrows. Each of these movements or combinations of these were meant to convey a diverse library of thoughts, emotions, and ideas.

For a deep dive into the entire vocabulary of Delsarte's system, you may want to pick up or download the book published in 1885 that was written and illustrated by Genevieve Stebbins.[9] There is an in-depth and detailed discussion of Delsarte's system and its uses in silent film performance in *Composing for Silent Film* by Jack Curtis Dubowsky.[10]

The gesture from the Delsarte method that you are probably most familiar with is one where the actor, wracked with anguish, clasps the back of their hand to their forehead. Buster Keaton spoofs this gesture in moments of mock grief during *The Scarecrow* (1920) and *The Goat* (1921). I have found that the gesturing Buster uses is so arcane to a modern audience that, for his send-up of this performing style to get over, I have to play a couple bars of schmaltzy melodrama-type music to help the audience out.

There are other gestures from this vocabulary that turn up in silent movies. Quite often, Chaplin has Edna Purviance make a loose fist and bite the forefinger of it when she needs to appear worried. In Keystone comedies, when Mabel Normand needs to indicate to us or to let someone in a scene know she is in love with "Fatty" Arbuckle, she will point to her heart, describe a pair of large parentheses in the air with her hands, then point to her ring finger.

---

[9] *Delsarte System of Expression* (Edgar S. Werner, 1885) and *Delsarte System of Dramatic Expression* (Edgar S. Werner, 1885), both by Genevieve Stebbins, are available on archive.org.
[10] *Composing for Silent Film* by Jack Curtis Dubowsky (Routledge Books, 2024). More than half of the first chapter, "Silent Film Conventions," covers this topic.

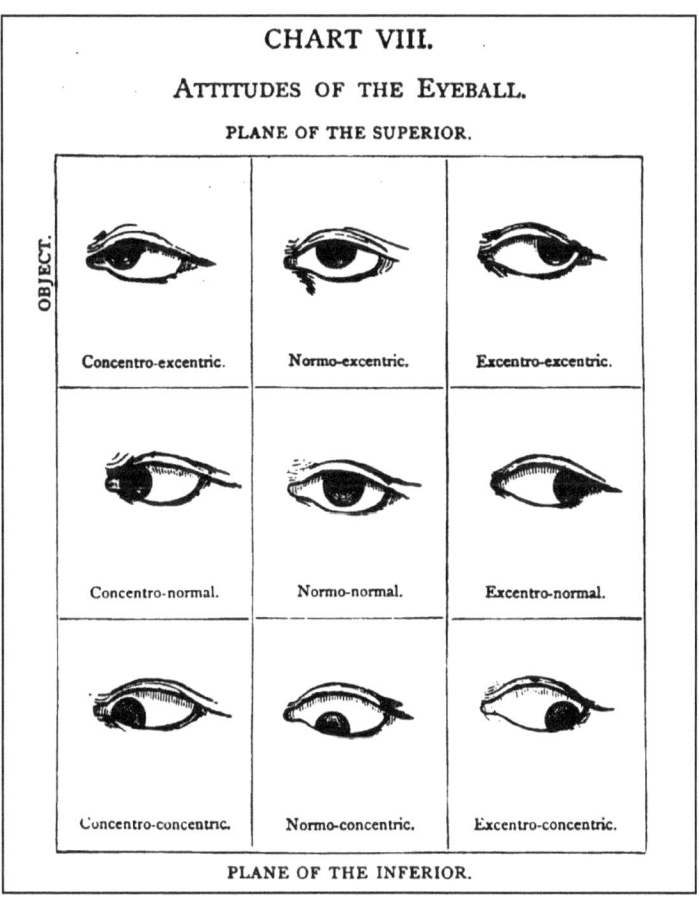

Illustration from Delsarte System of Dramatic Expression
(1885, Edgar S. Werner) by Genevieve Stebbins.

These are oversimplifications, of course, and the use of Delsarte gesturing is not rampant in early film, as many people assume. Just look at Griffith's *The New York Hat* (1912), or any number of his Biograph shorts from 1909–1910. Mary MacLaren's performance in *Shoes* (1916), directed by Lois Weber, is remarkably simple and nuanced, and is devoid of gesturing that telegraphs to us what she is thinking over. While the catalog of familiar-at-the-time gestures gradually disappears during the silent era, as acting techniques improve and actors find better and better ways of indicating without "indicating," this practice does not go away completely.

In a scene about halfway into King Vidor's *The Crowd* (1928), after the main characters John and Mary have had a big argument and John storms out to go to work, there is a very long and sustained take, during which Mary reacts to what has happened. Eleanor Boardman, who plays Mary, stands there and thinks through her situation. There is a moment when it occurs to her that she has some important and life-altering news she has not told John. At this point, she gently clutches her stomach, and we realize she is pregnant. This is purely for us. *She* knows she is pregnant. The gesture lets us know that, in her internal monologue, she has realized she has not told John yet.

There is a balancing act that has to happen in silent film performance in order to inform us what is in the characters' minds and what they are conveying to each other. Initially, the Delsarte catalog of gestures—which could certainly be choreographed to music in a dance, like the Electric Slide, the Macarena, or a line dance—was the go-to method.

• • •

In some early silent films, one of the main characters will face the camera, or at least what it appears they think is an audience, and talk through the screen's fourth wall. It is a theatrical device known well enough by audiences that it gets spoofed in the Marx Brothers' film *Animal Crackers* (1930). Groucho, in the middle of talking with Mrs. Whitehead and Mrs. Rittenhouse, turns to one of them and says, "Pardon me, while I have a 'Strange Interlude.'" He then takes a step toward us and delivers a brief soliloquy straight into the camera.[11] Silent film found a way to get around this type of monologuing during the early 1910s.

I had always been puzzled that comedian Ford Sterling never caught on to this in his many performances in Keystone shorts where he would stop, turn to the camera, and tell us that he knew what the other characters were plotting and he had an idea that would fix them, and then explain to us what that was—even though this was a silent movie, and none of what Sterling was mouthing and gesticulating is revealed in any intertitles. Then I realized that his character was spoofing a convention of stage melodrama that was well known to audiences of the time— namely, the sneering mustache-twirling villain of the play.

This device of a character in silent movies letting us know their cerebral machinations by telling us in words, and sometimes in gestures, came from a theatrical convention many moviegoers would have been familiar with. It was certainly helpful for cinema's initial melting-pot audience, for whom there was often a language barrier. This convention faded from use in film acting by the mid-1910s.

---

[11] Groucho is referencing Eugene O'Neill's 1928 play, which had been on Broadway concurrently with the Marx Brothers' *Animal Crackers*.

A title card that would read something like "Determined to stop the wedding, he purchases a harpoon" was a much more economical way of conveying information to the audience. It certainly had fewer words to translate, and it kept the film's forward motion and comedy going.

James Murray and Eleanor Boardman in King Vidor's *The Crowd* (1928).
(courtesy of Robert Arkus)

• • •

The movement and performance styles in silent films evolved during the 1910s and 1920s, becoming less theatrically rooted and more naturalistic, or at least authentic. A certain amount of this got adapted into a specific performance style, unique to silent film, which carried through to the end of the 1920s. How much of that is theatrical performance or distilled pantomime, and how much of it is silent film performance techniques?

A lot of theatrical conventions were accepted by or acceptable to moviegoing audiences during the silent era: the eyeliner, lipstick, pancake-white makeup applied just to the face and neck. The same goes for what we in hindsight think of as theatrical gestures and movement.

They may appear to be arcane or antiquated to us today and are often mistaken for "silent movie acting." But these conventions are what performers knew, and even the ones who had not spent years in vaudeville would pick up the rhythms and physicalities from fellow performers on the shooting stages or in rehearsals. Harold Lloyd, for example, was not a circus or vaudeville comedian originally—his performance experience had been on the legitimate stage. But Lloyd was an avid and dedicated learner, and by the time he had spent a year at Keystone and another year with Hal Roach as "Lonesome Luke"—absorbing Physical Comedy 101 from costar Snub Pollard—you would never know Lloyd had not spent years in vaudeville.

Part of the holding-on to the physical traits of theatrical performance is rooted in the need to be able to convey to the audience the beats in the scene and emotional moments or drama without the aid of speech. The economy of the movement style appears to develop during the early 1910s, when silent film's storytelling language was less reliant on mouthing lines of dialog or pointing to people or doors, and so forth. We are given just enough information so we can tell what is going on without lipreading and interpreting overt gestures. This, of course, was partnered with the support of occasional intertitles.

But strip away the Victorian-era physicality, and silent film performance is still possible. There is still a way to convey information, just enough of it, for the viewer to understand what is going on.

• • •

There is an aspect of physical performance in silent film that is unique to this medium and that allows the audience to understand what one character is saying to another. It is a form of gesture that is paired with spoken dialog (unheard by us) that lies somewhere between speaking as one normally would and charades-type pantomiming of words or phrases.

In 2018, I was in rehearsals for *The Final Reel*, a play that was being created and produced by Parallel Exit, a physical comedy theater company based in New York City.[12] The show takes place in the present, in an about-to-shutter vintage movie house where a fictional silent comedy feature—the long-missing last reel of which has been found and restored—is about to be shown. During one scene in the play, that silent film is shown, but during reel one something happens that is a cross between *Sherlock, Jr.* (1924) and *The Purple Rose of Cairo* (1985)— someone from the world of the movie house enters the film, and later brings someone from the world of the film back out into the cinema auditorium.

The silent movie in *The Final Reel* that is "projected" in the theater was performed live by the actors. I was cast

[12] *The Final Reel* was conceived by Mike Dobson, Joel Jeske, Mark Lonergan, and Scott McCord.

as Ben Model, the silent film accompanist who is the cinema's house pianist. I attended all the rehearsals, so that I could gradually build the score on the action, accompanying the performers while the scenes were being staged.

A moment came during rehearsal when the silent movie scenes had been blocked and set, with the performers saying their characters' lines out loud, and everyone in the cast knew what was going on during the scenes. Mark Lonergan, the show's director, then told us we had gotten to the point where—since this was a silent movie—everyone would have to stop talking. They would "speak," but could not make any sound.

Suddenly, everyone interacting with one another in the scenes had no way of knowing what each other meant when they were speaking nor what was going on. Nor would anyone watching.

What I was able to contribute at that moment is this performance-style hybrid that I have noticed. It is something unique to silent film, which dribbled over a little into early talkies in the actors who had been in silents for several years or more. And that is a technique of gently gesturing in a way that illustrates and/or reinforces what is being said.

Not the literal point-to-eye, cover-heart-with-hand, point-to-someone gesturing to mean "I love you," but a more scaled-down gesture or head move or combination of these. It is a way of gesturing that refers to the object or person being discussed or the action they are suggesting be taken. The spoken dialog still happens, but in real life you would not tap your wrist if you asked someone what time it is, or gesture over your shoulder if you were talking about something behind you. These simple movements convey enough that we can take in the gestures and facial expressions to figure out what is being discussed. Not too much, not too little...just the right amount. The rest we can conjure up in our imagination, recognizing the physical iconography and aligning it with pieces of our own human experience. The Silent Film Universe being what it is, we accept this as viewers.

I am sharing this anecdote about *The Final Reel* because friends and fans who saw the show told me that its staged film scenes really resembled what silent movies look like. Yes, the performers were dressed in shades of gray, and the projected intertitles used an authentic typeface, but what I believe sealed the deal was that the actors were employing this performance technique.

Now that I have pointed this out, as you continue to watch silent movies, you may start to become aware of this physical language. During the COVID pandemic, when we were wearing masks over our mouths and noses, I found myself unwittingly using this physical communication to help convey things to people, during a time when it was hard for us to hear each other and because the more expressive portion of our faces was covered.

• • •

This subtle miming to support what is being said or conveyed appears to have gotten itself set and codified by the mid-1910s. It did not change much for the rest of the silent era, aside from being used a little less, as needed. This reduction of gesturing may not have been done deliberately, but during the last fifteen years of the silent era, filmmakers and performers gradually left more to the audiences to assemble in their imaginations.

It is not like charades at all, although that is the first place people go when they think of pantomiming action (as opposed to *mime*), but it is one form of nonverbal communication that even today's audiences are able to easily comprehend.

These gestures held over into the early sound era, mainly with performers who had been in pictures for a long time. It is noticeable when they are in scenes with actors who were new to motion pictures in the early 1930s. The silent-era actors seem overly theatrical in some cases. Oliver Hardy brought this gesturing practice along with him into talkies, but it doesn't come off as stilted— his personality and charm makes it seem like an organic part of his character.

Actors who had been in movies only a few years when sound came in do not appear to exhibit this physicality. Stars like Norma Shearer or Ronald Colman rose to stardom in mid-1920s silents at a time when the movement away from this style of performance was already, slowly, occurring, and their 1930s films belie their having worked before the silent movie camera.

But during the silent era, this was the way people moved and let us in on what they were saying, and sometimes what they were thinking or plotting. It is a performance practice unique to silent film that relies on our using both hemispheres of our brain to take in the information we see and synthesize the rest of it. And it is another reason why silent film is a universal language.

Although this may be a form of gesturing that was developed for the silent screen and became outmoded decades ago, little bits of it survive in daily life today. Think of this the next time you get a restaurant server's attention to let them know you want the check, or if you watch a flight attendant's "performance" during the safety demonstration prior to takeoff.

9.

THE SPEED(S) OF SILENT FILM

Up to this point I have covered all the aspects of silent film that are easily visually recognizable. Some of the finer points of performance style or technique may be new to you. Now that they have been identified, they can be readily noticed in the viewing of silent movies as much as the other facets I have described.

There is, however, one element of the Silent Film Universe that has gone unnoticed and under-researched, and is to a great degree misunderstood. That element is the speed—or rather, the *speed-up*—of silent film.

This unique property of pre-talking moving pictures is one I believe is not only important but is one of the medium's essential elements. It is one that evaporated in a puff of smoke with the talkie transition. The practice of what this technique was and how it was used disappeared and was almost never spoken of again.

Because this facet has not been researched, explored, discussed, or written about extensively before, this segment of the book will be something of a mega-chapter, broken down into sections. The various components of what I understand as being the speed-up of silent film had no precedent, since they formed during the middle years of the silent era. Because the need for and use of this performance/camera technique ended when silent movies did, its practices and methods were instantly forgotten about. There is a lot to be covered here, because this realm of the Silent Film Universe has never been part of conversations or studies of the medium.

What I have discovered may be revelatory for you. The first time I gave a lecture (with video clips) on this topic, David Robinson—film historian and author of *Chaplin: His Life and Art* (1985, McGraw Hill)— said to me, "How did we *miss* this all these years?"

What we missed was something that I noticed about the way silent movies look.

I knew back in my high-school days of Super 8mm filmmaking that silent movies were shown at a faster frames-per-second rate than the one they were filmed at. When I made a couple of silent movie shorts back then, I set my movie camera to 18 fps and projected the film at 24 fps. My amateur films' sped-up playback kind of resembled or reminded me of what I had seen in silent movies. But it didn't look *precisely* like the silents I had been obsessed with since childhood. I have found this to be the same with other filmmakers' post-1929 silents.

During the first decade of the 2000s, I began accompanying more and more silent film shows, and by the following decade this work became what I did for a living. Consequently, I spent more of my conscious, unconscious, and subconscious time thinking about silent films and their presentation. I developed a fascination, one that deepened over time, with projection speeds as employed at shows I was doing at a variety of venues. My interest in understanding this speed or speed-up phenomenon of silent cinema was focused on what made it happen and, eventually, how it was practiced on set and in cinemas during the silent era. This led me to a series of deconstruction efforts...and then a revelation.

I figured out what this "secret sauce" of the look of silent movies was and what its formulas were. I was then able to corroborate my hunches with research, through deconstructing shots and scenes from silent movies and through performing some silent-filmmaking experimentation. I have come to refer to what I have discovered about the speed-up of silent film as "undercranking." The term already existed, mainly in sound-era applications, but I thought it was a good fit for what I had figured out about the way silent movies were made and presented.

• • •

THE CONUNDRUM OF SILENT FILM SPEEDS

Here is the quasi-paradox that intrigued me:

If you run film (or video) faster than normal speed, the result is just that—it looks like footage that has been sped up. However...

Silent film is projected at faster-than-taking speed, and yet it doesn't look that way. Everything registers, clearly, as if the film was not sped up at all.

I'll say that again.

When you run film faster than normal speed...it looks *too fast*.

Silent film *is* run faster than normal speed…and it looks *fine*.

Let's start off with the assumption that what we see when we watch silent movies is correct, as far as the faster projection speed and the movement not looking too fast. After all, silent movies released with recorded scores in the late 1920s look this way, as do the two silent films Charlie Chaplin made after the talkie transition.

That familiar speed-up is present in silents released with a synchronized score, such as F. W. Murnau's *Sunrise* (1927)—which Murnau really wanted to be shown at 100 feet a minute, or 27 fps—and it's there in *The Better 'Ole* (1926), *Old San Francisco* (1927), and *Lonesome* (1928), among others, and in the silent portions of part-talkies released in 1928–29.

This look, clearly, was what audiences during the silent era were used to. Warner Brothers wasn't throwing America a major curveball in 1926 when they released the silent *Don Juan* with a recorded synchronized musical score and some sound effects. The film was a big, high-profile super-production starring John Barrymore. The big premiere event—held at Warners' largest and grandest theater in Manhattan—opened with a program of sync-sound Vitaphone short films. These shorts, unlike *Don Juan*, were all filmed at the same speed as they were to be projected at. They had to be, as they were sync-sound "talkie" shorts of performances of both classical and popular music by premier artists.

If this "silent movie" look I am referring to *was* incorrect, Warner Brothers would have had to go back and reshoot *Don Juan* with the cameras running at the same speed the projectors were now locked in to for sound— 90 feet per minute, or 24 frames per second. But they didn't, which tells us that this "look" of silent film is what audiences of the time saw and were used to. The same was the case for the people who made the films.

The first time I saw *The Jazz Singer* (1927), I was surprised that—except for Jolson's musical numbers—it was actually a silent movie, and it had that same silent film speed-up I was used to seeing.

Mary Astor and John Barrymore in *Don Juan* (1926).
(courtesy of Robert Arkus)

If silent film was supposed to be shown at the same speed it was filmed at, Charlie Chaplin, knowing that *City Lights* (1931) would be shown at 24 fps, would have shot the entire film at 24 fps. I have seen studio records from the film's production, and they list camera speeds for every take—and they are either 16 or 18 fps…but mostly 16. There are a few shots that say "10-14 fps," indicating that Chaplin's longtime cameraman Rollie Totheroh started the take cranking at 14 and dropped down to 10 for a specific effect, or the other way around. Chaplin and Totheroh filmed *Modern Times* (1936) the same way, and filming records for that picture bear this out.

• • •

You may have encountered two minor aberrations of this look of silent movies I am discussing. More common is the appearance of silent film that *does* look too fast—or lies somewhere between what I have outlined and seeming too fast. The other instance is silents that look like they are being shown too slowly.

Yes, sometimes silent movies are run too fast, faster than they ought to be, faster than they would have been originally presented in their original run. Some of them, anyway. For a long time after the silent era, there were not any options to vary the projection rate to replicate the film's original projection speed, and this appearing-too-fast state either became something sound-era fans got accustomed to or it became a stereotype about silent movies that could be off-putting.

The rate at which sound film is projected was locked, in 1925, at 90 feet per minute, or 24 frames per second. Once talking pictures took over from silents in 1929, projectors in theaters no longer had rheostats on them for adjusting projection speed up or down as there had always been for silent pictures. Not only was this the case for theatrical 35mm projectors, it was also the case for 16mm projectors used in schools and homes, and for telecine (film transfer) equipment used by television stations to broadcast motion picture film, usually in 16mm.

Starting in the 1930s, silent movies were seen—when they were seen—at this one "sound film" frame rate of 24 fps. This generated the "herky-jerky" stereotype of silent film that people think of. Not all silent movies, just the films made in the 1910s and maybe early 1920s, have this too-much-espresso look to them.

• • •

At the time of the publication of this book, four decades have elapsed since I began accompanying silent films. I have played to hundreds and hundreds of them, in a wide variety of venues and in a variety of film and video formats, and always with an audience—except for recordings done for home video. One thing I have noticed, and that my film accompanist colleagues have noticed as well, is that when a silent movie is being shown "too slow," it's more work for the accompanist.

I don't know what this inner metronome is and how I developed it or what it is based on. You may have experienced the same thing, and many people have their own opinions on the "right speed" to show silent movies. What it feels like for the accompanist is that more effort is needed to create or support the film's drama and forward-motion energy. It is as if you are not only playing the piano, but also pushing it across the floor.

I had known what "too slow" seemed like to me, and many of my friends had similar opinions. What stuck in my mind—the question mark over my head, if you will— is *why* the films seemed too slow. The rule of thumb with slapstick shorts I developed years ago is that if the laughs are not there during a theatrical screening when they are usually present, you know the running speed is not right.

In the same way that silent film can be over-sped in projection, with variable-speed projection as an option there is also the possibility of a film being run a bit slower than it ought to be. This can be pretty subjective. But— as with over-speeding—if there is some knowledge about the film's year of release and the average speeds films were presented at that year, this can be corrected.

It can also get ignored because—to the person choosing a running speed for a given screening—a film may look *to them* like the people onscreen are running around like the Keystone Kops (a phrase I have heard many programmers and film curators use to describe this).

What is it that makes the film seem like it's a tad gooey, or running "too slow"? A lot of this comes from what one is used to in watching silent films, both dramas and comedies. Some of us have seen these films for decades, always shown at "sound speed," and we are used to the speed-up, and expect it. So did movie audiences in the 1920s.

Many people think of 16 or 18 fps as "silent speed," and that it applies to all silent movies. I have a theory about where this term came from and how it got affixed to this projection rate. I will address that later in this chapter.

These viewings of silent films where they seem too fast or too slow are related to the "look" of silent film I have described above as being the norm. So, then, if most silents have this look, why is that some silents look faster, and what is it about running them slower that seems slightly "off"?

•   •   •

Having had the opportunity to accompany silent films at MoMA (the Museum of Modern Art) in New York for many years, I learned that their projectors were *variable*-speed, and that films shown in their cinemas could be run at a variety of speeds instead of the either/or of 24 fps or 18 fps. I had a lot of chances to see which speeds worked best for films made during different years, and gradually got to have input on the running speed of a film I was going to accompany.

What I noticed over years of doing shows is that silent films from different parts of the silent era look and seem "fine" when run at 24 fps, and some do not. It seemed that films from the early 1910s held up best at a rate of 18 fps, from the mid-1910s at a range from 18 to 21, from the early 1920s at 20 to 22, and then from around 1923 on, 24 fps seemed fine. The further back you went, the slower the projection speed needed to be (or vice versa).

By "looked fine" I mean that there is a certain amount of decoding we in the audience are required to do in viewing the films. What I noticed with films from the 1910s (when projected too fast) is that when they were run at a more hospitable speed a lot of facial expression and reactions became visible and decodable. When over-speeding a film from the 1910s, these reactions—information we are being given and need to take in, specifically the motivation or reason a character onscreen does something—can get erased. The film zips by, leaving only the physical action the decision has precipitated. This creates the impression of people "running around like the Keystone Kops."

For decades, the only way to see Keystone shorts from 1914–1916 was in editions shown on TV run at 24 fps. I have had many opportunities to watch Keystone shorts projected at 20 or 21 fps and have noticed that at that rate the slapstick still lands, but the character's *decision* to throw those bricks (it's always bricks, and very rarely pies) is apparent to us. Not like in a stage production of an Ibsen play, but just enough so the films don't play like a Punch and Judy puppet show.

Conversely, films from the 1920s shown at a frame rate below 24 fps can seem a tad sluggish. They don't quite have the same energy as they do when projected at "sound speed," and comedies don't feel like they have their usual "snap."

My realization that there was this gradual shift in silent films' being less (or more) decodable from 1908 to 1929—if your only option is to watch them at one projection speed—was one of the clues that triggered the next part of my exploration of filming and projection speeds in silent film.

• • •

Okay, so if there is an established "look" to silent movies that "feels right," then why do dramatic silents feel sluggish at a certain projection speed and "better" at a slightly faster one? Why does projection speed have the same effect with comedies, making their gags land better and get their laughs…or not? This is the quest I went on once I had come up with a basic but thorough idea of which projection speeds for silents seemed "right."

Perhaps it is my background in filmmaking—which has run concurrently with my interest in silent films and music—that led me to what I have turned up. Going down the rabbit hole of trying to understand what it was like for the people who made these films, what the process was for them and what really happened on set, is what eventually led to my discovering, understanding, and grasping what this "look" of silent film is, how it works, and how it was executed.

The speed-up of silent film certainly appears to have been a given, something understood and accepted as a norm. The films did not have to be run faster than taking speed…but they *could* be. And they were. There were issues on the filmmaking end because of the light sensitivity of the film itself, and cranking cameras faster meant the shutter might not let in enough light for a proper exposure. Cranking a bit faster would also use up more film, adding cost to the production. In the cinemas, there was also flicker that needed to be avoided, and this dictated minimum speeds.

Additionally, theater owners would run their program at whatever speed they needed or wanted to in order to maintain their schedule. If a film was run faster, the show would end sooner, and an additional one could be fit into the schedule. (Or the projectionist could go home a little earlier.) If the theater manager had a set number of shows to present every day and the next feature that came in was nine or ten reels long and not six or seven, projection speed was a factor to consider.

My observation is that in silent film, the entire film— every shot—was filmed with these two different speed standards for the same entertainment product, that all silent movies were shown in theaters at a slightly faster speed than the one(s) at which they had been filmed (or cranked).

There is a reason silent film does not look like film that is running faster, even though it *is*. That reason is what I am referring to as "undercranking."

• • •

With motion picture film, the way to speed up what you are watching is to run the camera more slowly than it would normally be run.

In sound-era or contemporary film, undercranking was often used in some shots during car chase sequences. Filming this way allowed the drivers to execute certain stunts a little more safely by driving at a slower speed. Driving at 35 miles an hour can be made to appear on-screen like the car is moving at 50 miles an hour when the shot is undercranked.

In sound-era films, undercranking has been used to emulate a silent movie look or to make something look silly, since the sped-up look resembles what many people think of when it comes to silent movies. The result is that the action moves faster, and does look sillier, although it does not quite look the way silent film does—running faster without appearing that way.

• • •

It's the difference between any silent movie made before 1930—especially with comedies and action films—and what you see in sound films or sequences that are supposed to be "silent movie-ish." There are undercranked sped-up bits in some shots in Stanley Kramer's *It's a Mad, Mad, Mad, Mad World* (1963), in director Richard Lester's films from the 1960s, in slapstick sequences on *The Benny Hill Show* (1955–1989) or *The Goodies* (1970–1982), or even in something like the opening title sequence of the sitcom *The Fresh Prince of Bel Air* (1990–1996).

If you really look closely, you will notice the difference between silent era film and any other, later, use of the speed-up.

You may have also noticed a similar sped-up look in some films from the 1930s. Boxing scenes in early 1930s films were often undercranked, like the ones in *The Champ* (1931) with Wallace Beery. Sometimes just one shot, or even just a piece of one, would be sped up to boost the impact of a punch or a fall. The shot that ends the stateroom scene in the Marx Brothers film *A Night at the Opera* (1935), when everyone tumbles out into the ship's hallway, comes to mind. There are similar uses in Laurel & Hardy and Three Stooges shorts. Sometimes this was achieved through undercranking during filming, and sometimes the effect was achieved after the fact in the studio's film lab, as it was in the Marx Brothers film.

I had always noticed these uses, and it was obvious to me that there was something different between these and silent movies. It just looked like the action was going faster than normal. But I was intrigued with the idea that silent movies had a specific look to them, as far as the onscreen action and movement was concerned. You may have noticed as well.

I have approached my research on this filmmaking facet of silent film by trying to have an empathic under-standing of what it was like to *make* these motion pictures. I thought a lot about what the cameramen, film cutters, directors, and actors were expecting of the way the films were going to be shown in movie theaters—as part of their creative process—when it came to utilizing this dif-ference between taking speeds and projection speeds.

It is unclear precisely when actors and directors in si-lent movies started using this technique. But what I have noticed, from watching and accompanying silent movies for so many years, is that it does appear to be ubiquitous in practice from a certain point in the early or mid-1910s through the rest of the silent era.

There isn't much documentary evidence in trade mag-azines or in interviews with veterans of the silent era, but I have turned up a few smoking guns. I am now certain that what we see and what I have discovered about silent film as far as cranking speeds and performance techniques is a deliberate practice, one that everyone was in on. I have figured out how it works, both in theory and in practice.

So, then, what was happening on set, on the shooting stages, that created this effect that does not look like film-running-too-fast?

For me, what unlocked all of this was a film Chaplin made in the silent era and then presented, in a reissue, in the sound era.

•   •   •

A DECONSTRUCTION AND A REVELATION

At some point when I was in college or somewhere in my twenties, I saw *The Chaplin Revue* (1959) at the Carnegie Hall Cinema, one of several revival houses that used to be in Manhattan. Lee Erwin accompanied the film on the theater's Wurlitzer organ, and that was the main reason I had attended the show. I had befriended Lee when I began playing the piano for silents at film history classes at NYU while majoring in film production there.

Something about the Chaplin film, one scene in particular, stuck with me for years.

Charlie Chaplin released *The Chaplin Revue* two years after the release of *A King in New* York (1957) and seven after *Limelight* (1952). The "Revue" was composed of three of Chaplin's silent comedy shorts: *A Dog's Life* (1918), *Shoulder Arms* (1918), and *The Pilgrim* (1923). They had new musical scores by Chaplin, and *The Pilgrim* even had a western cowboy song, "Bound for Texas," written by Chaplin and sung by pop singer Matt Monro, as part of its soundtrack.

The Chaplin Revue was released around the time that silent movies' first renaissance was beginning to take off and people were being exposed to silents again. The three years following Chaplin's anthology film saw the releases of Robert Youngson's silent film compilation features *When Comedy Was King* (1960) and *Days of Thrills and Laughter* (1961) as well as the broadcast of the Killiam Shows TV series *Silents, Please!* (1960–1962), which showcased classics of the silent screen in half-hour abridgments.

The singing-cowboy song wasn't the only thing in *The Chaplin Revue* that was trying to appeal or cater to an audience of the time. There was something else, something nearly omnipresent throughout the film: the three Chaplin shorts were step-printed.

Step-printing, sometimes referred to as stretch-printing, is a process done with a motion picture optical printer to adjust the perceived viewing speed of a film. By printing every second or third frame of film twice, a film can be made to appear to be running slower than 24 frames per second. This is the way most video editing programs slow footage down, by digitally duplicating frames.

Chaplin was not the only silent film star concerned that their films might be considered by the general public to be "olde tyme flickers" and would get laughed at for the wrong reason, or seen as silly or maudlin. Harold Lloyd removed scenes from some of his films in preparing his compilation reissues. In preparing *Harold Lloyd's Funny Side of Life* (1963), Lloyd cut the moment at the end of the big party scene in *The Freshman* (1925) when his character breaks down and cries. Mary Pickford had planned to destroy all her films in the 1930s, but fortunately Lillian Gish talked her out of it.

This concern about showing silent movies at a slower frame rate to a 1950s or 1960s audience brings me to *The Chaplin Revue* and its step-printing. The shorts in the *Revue* were reproduced with every other frame printed twice, replicating the look of their being presented at 16 frames per second, at which the movement of the performers was at or close to "natural speed." (I will discuss this somewhat subjective notion of "natural movement" later.)

Film that has been step-printed appears to have a very slight movement jitter—which you get used to—and the physical movements are a lot closer to real-time speed.

What I noticed about the speed at the screening of *The Chaplin Revue* I attended was not only that the films seemed slow and to lack the usual "snap" or energy, but there was something else that wasn't quite right. The Charlie I saw in the films, especially in one particular sequence in *A Dog's Life*, was not the Charlie I knew and loved. There was something that was slightly off, or missing, in this slowed-to-natural-speed edition of the film.

•　•　•

In the sequence from *A Dog's Life* that takes place in an employment office, Charlie has been sitting on a bench with several other men, waiting to be called up to the window to be given a work assignment. Charlie is closest to the clerk's window at the front of the office. Cut to a close-up of the window, and a man (played by Charles Reisner) steps into view and gestures for the applicants to approach the window. Charlie hops up from the bench.

As Charlie walks toward the window, one of the other men, from the other end of the bench, gets up and briskly walks past Charlie and arrives at the window before Charlie can. This happens again, and again and again.

The little man with the baggy pants and toothbrush mustache, however, seemed unaware that this was happening. It was almost as if he were allowing it to happen, over and over. The other men just walk right past him and get to the window before Charlie does.

This made him come off as more slow-witted than the Charlie I knew from so many years of watching his movies. The Charlie I knew was cleverer than this and would have caught on and solved the problem. His physical comedy was always more about split-second timing and physical grace and agility. Charlie should have been the one zipping ahead of the other men as each of them approached the clerk at the window, if not the first time then perhaps after one or two failed attempts.

So, what was going on here? Chaplin would not have created some business that was out of character. And not just out of character…it wasn't that funny, or not as funny as it ought to be. Nor was a sequence later in the film with Charlie and his brother Sydney, as a proprietor of a lunch wagon, when Charlie keeps snatching biscuits from a tray and stuffing them in his mouth when Syd has his back turned.

Charlie Chaplin in *A Dog's Life* (1918).
(copyright © Roy Export S.A.S.)

A couple decades after I attended that screening, I got my hands on a DVD of *The Chaplin Revue* and was able to try something I had always wanted to see—speeding up the film.

It had always appeared to be running a little too slow at the step-printed rate that was approximating 16 fps. As it turned out, there was more at play here than just the overall speed.

• • •

I ripped the file from the DVD and brought it into iMovie, which had timing controls that would make a video clip play back slower or faster. I sped the Chaplin footage up a little.

Bingo!

Not only did the sequence "look right," but two things were now in place: the business was *funny*, and I was now seeing the Charlie Chaplin I *knew*. Rather than seemingly and stupidly letting each of the other men step in front of him over and over, what I now saw was the Little Tramp earnestly walking briskly to the window, and each time someone zipped in front of him at the last instant, snagging the job offered at the window. This was then capped by the clown business of his being caught up in the routine of dashing back and forth, repeating the action even after there were no jobs left and no more men running up to the window.

How did this happen? How was this suddenly a Charlie Chaplin physical comedy routine where moments before…it *wasn't?*

The answer came in an answer to the next thing I wondered: what did the movement look like when the film was being made, in real time?

Knowing of my interest in cranking speeds in silent films, David Totheroh—grandson of Chaplin's cameraman—had sent me a copy of an interview that he and his father conducted with Rollie in 1964, one that had been published in a 1972 issue of *Film Culture*. In the conversation, Rollie discussed specific frame rates used in taking the scenes in Chaplin's silent comedy shorts, citing 14 fps and 12 fps as typical cranking speeds, and saying that prior to working for Chaplin 16 fps would have been typical for drama.

Remembering this, I realized I knew how to view the footage at cranking speed. Doing some quick math, knowing the step-printed footage was emulating a projection speed of 16 fps, I slowed the video file playback so it appeared to be running at 14 fps.

What was now revealed in the real-time viewing was that Chaplin was deliberately allowing the other performers to get in front of him. He did not seem to be in that much of a hurry to get to the clerk's window, and each time the routine was executed the other actor walked a little more briskly than Chaplin and easily slipped in front of him. So—this was all specifically choreographed, in terms of the movement speed of the performers, so that when projected faster the effect would make it look like Charlie was moving briskly, and somehow the other men would zip in front of him without his even being aware of it.

111

This was my big light-bulb-over-the-head moment, when I realized that silent film was not just the slightly faster projection speed, but that it was a combination— really a collaboration—of performance and that speed-up. What dawned on me was that the people making the films definitely *knew* the film would be shown faster in theaters and *utilized* the speed-up by moving or creating movement at a different and specific pace for it.

This is the very reason that silent film does not merely look the way regular film or video does when it is run faster.

• • •

Dissecting this gag in Chaplin's *A Dog's Life* pulled back the curtain on the sleight-of-hand "magic" of this speed-up phenomenon I had noticed and revealed to me what that secret was. Why it had not occurred to me before was also fascinating, because it made complete sense.

Of *course*, the people who made movies knew the films were being shown at a faster speed in theaters. Even if they did not regularly see their own pictures, they certainly saw others' and discussed them with each other—not just the actors, but also the cameramen and directors and writers. They all knew what speed they were cranking at on set and what speed films were being shown at.

I have found documentation on the two sets of film speeds, one for "taking" and one for projection—not lots, but enough, and every once in a while another nugget turns up. While it is unclear how this unique facet of silent film happened, it seems to have become pretty standard by the mid-1910s.

The more I looked at silent film comedies at cranking speed, slowing down video of silent film sequences over and over, the more I saw exactly what I had seen in the footage that Chaplin had had step-printed in 1959. This was, namely, the choice and technique of the performers to move at a pace that compensated for the speed-up. I also noticed the utilization of another aspect of performance, something that I believe is unique to the medium of silent film, and which must have come from a pair of stage-performance techniques.

The first—one that fascinated me the most, and continues to—is an application of sleight-of-hand to physical performance. Again, I have no idea how or when this was realized, but it is the secret to the difference between Charlie appearing to stupidly let each of the men cut in front of him over and over, and Charlie having these same people get the best of him, neatly scooting ahead of him in a split second.

The speed-up of silent film creates an elision of time when there are quick movements. These brisk movements appear even quicker, especially when they are played against other performers' slightly slower movements. Chaplin, ensemble player Henry Bergman, and the rest of the comedians in this scene knew that if cameraman Rollie Totheroh was cranking at 14 fps, and Charlie was walking at the pace that he was and the other men were moving at the speed they were, Charlie could—in real time—carefully allow them to get in front of him just as he was approaching the clerk window. They did so with the knowledge that when the film was projected at 80 feet per minute or 20 fps,[13] the speed-up would create the illusion that the men were suddenly slipping in front of Charlie, so quickly that he could not catch a break no matter how many times he tried.

It was a physical gag that *only* existed in the slightly sped-up universe of silent film. It is analogous to the way a magician practices a sleight-of-hand maneuver repeatedly so that one part of their prestidigitation happens rapidly enough that the coin or card in their hand seems to appear or disappear, as if "by magic."

• • •

CONFIRMATION, IN PRACTICE AND IN RESEARCH

Once I discovered or realized this notion that people making silent comedies, and silent film in general, were *aware* of the difference between taking speeds and projection speeds, I became fascinated with finding more and more examples to see what this looked like when deconstructed. This became the basis for several "undercranking" videos I made and posted to YouTube.

I also wanted to try experimenting with the filmmaking-for-speed-up process itself. Luckily, I knew some clowns. Physical comedy performers know and are trained in the movement style we are familiar with from silent comedies, because it has the same roots in circus performance going back generations.

---

[13] This projection speed is one I have determined was in use for silent comedy shorts in the mid-to-late 1910s, from research and from observing audience reactions while accompanying films at hundreds of shows over many years.

There is a thriving circus, clown, and variety arts community in New York City, and over several years I have gotten to connect and become friends with some of these creators and performers. Many of them are silent comedy film fans who came to shows that I accompanied, and because of my own interest in the physical "how" of making silent comedy I gravitated to performances of groups like the Bindlestiff Family Cirkus, The New York Goofs, Parallel Exit, and others.

Silent filmmaking experiments that I did with folks from the circus world yielded further proof that my undercranking theories were right. I would get together with a couple of my clown friends, and they would concoct a very basic physical routine. I would film this digitally, and then play the footage back for all of us to watch—slightly sped up—via a camcorder-to-MacBook arrangement. Not double-speed, but approximating the 1.3–1.5x speed-up I had seen in silent comedies.

What we would see in the first take would initially look like footage running faster than normal. We would come up with adjustments to the physical tempos, and also insert very slight pauses between beats of movements, then take the scene again. We would watch it again, sped up. We would do this over and over, making still more adjustments. And then after about six or seven takes, something amazing happened.

What we had done looked exactly like a silent film.

Our video was sped up 50 percent, but everything read and could be decoded just as it would have been had the physical business been performed live, in real time and without the adjustments—all because the performers were moving slightly slower, which the speed-up acclimatized back into a new version of normal movement. The speed-up also erased or elided the pauses we had inserted, pauses which gave clearer delineation to the movement and which—in tandem with the slightly slower overall movement—kept the faster footage looking like, well…footage running too fast.

It was magic.

Over the ensuing few years I continued making these experiments with similar results as part of my participation in the NYC Physical Comedy Lab, which was organized by clown educator John Towsen. By this time, I was using an iPhone app called Filmic Pro, which allows you to select the frames-per-second rate for the capturing and for the playback of your footage. We could "crank" at 12, 14, 16, 18, and so forth, and then, right away, watch our gags played back at 24 fps. The process I had come up with was akin to the Jerry Lewis video assist,[14] but with the addition of the ability to monitor the trial and error of the speed-up everyone in the silent era was dealing with.

One of my clown friends, Jeff Seal, said something about the process and what his movement and performance felt like during that sixth or seventh "magic" take that answered another question, one I hadn't thought to consider. But it made complete sense. He said that the

---

[14] While making *The Bellboy* (1960), his directorial debut, Jerry Lewis utilized a video camera and videotape playback to watch himself in the film's takes. Although Lewis may not have been the very first to utilize this, the "Jerry Lewis video assist" is a nickname for the system, and I am using it here because we were using Filmic Pro for the same purpose Lewis had.

way he had performed and moved and made adjustments in that last take felt just like it did when he performed in a very large theater or circus, where your movements really had to read for people who were far away from you.

What this made me consider was the fact that everyone in silent movies had come from the theater, as well as circus or vaudeville and, in the case of European clowns, the music hall. They were used to this kind of physicality, one that would have to work in a theater that seated several hundred or a few thousand people. The same applies for performers of drama. So, when this idea of adjusting movements in front of a moving picture camera to compensate for the speed-up that was happening in movie theaters was hatched, the physicality did not have to be invented. It was already in everyone's bones and muscle memory.

•   •   •

Two published articles on screen acting bookending the silent era prove that the adjustment of physical movements for the motion picture camera was a known practice. One piece is from the mid-1910s, describing an experience that came just at the very end of the nickelodeon era, and the other was penned just prior to the talkie changeover.

In doing research on this performance technique, I had searched terms like "feet per minute," "minutes per reel," and "cranking" on the Lantern search engine harnessed to the online Media History Digital Library, and had come up with very little. A couple of minor tidbits, but not much. But I had never searched for the term "slow-motion acting." Why would I?

And yet it is one of the topics in an interview with Maurice Costello in a 1914 issue of *Movie Pictorial*. Terry Chester Shulman had turned up this article while researching his book *Film's First Family: The Untold Story of the Costellos* (2018, University Press of Kentucky), and let me know about it.

In the article, the interviewer asked Maurice Costello, regarding his start in motion pictures, "Did you find the motion picture acting at all difficult?"

"If you recall the early days of motion pictures," Mr. Costello explained, "you'll remember that the crude cameras and projecting machines of six years ago did not agree with the style of motion picture acting then in vogue. The acting looked terribly swift, jerky, and unconvincing when it was focused upon the screen. The first time that I saw myself on the films I could have torn out my hair. I kept wondering if I had looked like that through the years that I had been playing in stock. I asked my friends and my family. They were reassuring but the pictures weren't. I was playing only extra parts with the Vitagraph Company on a summer engagement and I didn't know much of the mechanics of the business. But I finally figured out that slow movement of the actors would help in giving the correct effects. The first chance I had I used it. When the picture was shown on trial the manager sent for me. I went, thinking that I was to have a reprimand for having introduced the novelty. That would have been the way of a theatrical manager. That's where I discovered the first advantage of the motion pictures. The Vitagraph Company made me their first leading man. I've been with them here ever since."[15]

[15] Interview with Maurice Costello, *Movie Pictorial*, July 25, 1914, 9.

This technique is something Costello became known for and, as Shulman goes on to describe, was credited for in other publications years later. What's striking to me is that Costello was describing this in 1914 and mentioning the cameras and projectors "of six years ago" and "the first time I saw myself on the films." Which means that he noticed this in 1908 or thereabout, and at some point, realized there was a way to counteract the speed-up he was seeing in theaters. He had recognized that the physicality workaround that he took a flier on made his performances in moving pictures *land* and *read* properly, thereby allowing his craft and expressiveness to register better than that of his fellow screen performers.

No wonder Vitagraph made him their leading man. The word must have spread. There is no documentation of that, but watching a lot of early-1910s films shows that Maurice Costello is not the only player or performer who adopted this slow-motion technique to their acting and movement. The folks at Keystone certainly caught on to this and ran with it.

By the end of the silent era, and probably sooner than that, it was second nature to everyone in pictures.

•   •   •

Milton Sills was a huge star during the silent era. Sills's name and face may be unfamiliar today, but he would have been an ideal "get" for Encyclopedia Britannica to write about screen acting techniques for its 14th edition, published in 1929. And not a moment too soon—talking pictures were about to change everything, and Sills himself passed away unexpectedly in 1930.

Milton Sills in *The Spoilers* (1923). Sills was a major dramatic star throughout the silent film era, although he and his films are very much forgotten today.

In a brief section of the encyclopedia article whose subhead is "Future Possibilities," Sills ruminates on what the talking picture might entail as far as performance techniques. Given the speculative nature of how he was discussing talkies, it is quite likely that he was writing his piece in 1928. But he had been a leading man in more than eighty feature-length films since the late 1910s, after having played one of the leads in the popular 1917 serial *Patria*, which starred Irene Castle.

So, he had a ton of experience under his belt to back up what he laid down on paper at what turned out to be the end of the silent era. Sills's article on motion picture acting is several pages long, covering many different aspects of production, actors' techniques, and how they relate to one another. But halfway down the right-hand column on page 861, Milton Sills spelled out in black and white what I had been seeing in my deconstructions of silent film segments, as far as taking speeds, projection speeds, and the way performers were compensating for the difference between them.

> While the normal speed of the camera in filming a performance is 16 pictures per second, or 60 ft. of film per minute, when the picture is projected in a theatre, it is the custom to run it at the rate of 24 pictures per second, or 90 ft. per minute. This, together with the fact that the film does not record movement as adequately as the eye, makes it necessary for the actor to adopt a more deliberate tempo than that of the stage or of real life. He must learn to time his action in accordance with the requirements of the camera, making it neither too fast nor too slow—a process of education only to be acquired through experience in the studio. The first mark of a novice is the rapidity and jerkiness of his movements, registered upon the screen as blurred and meaningless streaks. Another essential feature of the screen actor's technique is a careful spacing of significant items which constitute the sequence of the scene. One thing and one thing only must be done at a time, and this in a clean-cut and distinct style with no distracting, irrelevant or unnecessary movements.[16]

---

[16] Milton Sills, "Motion Picture Acting," *Encyclopedia Britannica*, 14th ed. (1929), 861.

The feet-per-minute numbers Sills uses are a bit of an oversimplification. Different scenes or shots could be and were (to my eye) taken at a variety of speeds, depending on the action or mood. By 1928, 18 fps or even 20 fps was a pretty typical cranking speed. Also, projection speeds were not regulated or locked down. Research I have done has found that by 1926 or 1927, 100 feet per minute (or approximately 27 fps) was a typical running speed. It was even faster in some of the smaller houses.

Typical projection speeds had started out in the early-to-mid-1910s at 16-18 fps (and camera cranking speeds slower than that). For reasons I have not been able to uncover, cranking and projection speeds had both been gradually creeping up over the ensuing eight to ten years.

But still, Milton Sills's declaration in the encyclopedia about How This Works confirms what Maurice Costello had discovered two decades prior: that moving pictures were taken at one speed and projected at a faster one. More importantly—and this is the smoking gun, trade-secret part—performers were aware of and were compensating for this by adjusting the way they were moving.

This performance technique is precisely what makes silent film look the way it does.

This is why silent films made somewhere in the early 1910s onward should be viewed faster than taking speed, even if the speed-up amount is minor—whether projected on film or rendered digitally. People who made movies then were expecting this increased speed to be present in cinemas and had this awareness in mind when making the films…so they would look "right" for audiences.

●　●　●

The "deliberate tempo" Milton Sills writes of was one of two things I picked up on when I began watching silent comedy film sequences at "cranking speed."[17] The slightly slower physical movement style is the one giveaway that most people pick up on when a silent movie is projected at a slower rate than was expected by the people who made the film, and, consequently, the speed at which it ought to be shown.

But there is something else that makes the overall performances seem slightly slower. It is something that almost gives a slightly mechanical look to the movement. This performance facet reminded me of something I learned from taking a semester of mime in college.

In the mime course, one of the things we were taught was to physically define the invisible object we were taking hold of. Not just outlining it, physically suggesting the shape of the object with the movements of our hand and fingers, but—more importantly—separating that object definition from what we next did with the object. There is a fraction of a second's pause you need to insert between grabbing the invisible mug's invisible handle and

---

[17] My estimation of what cranking speed was used on a given shot or sequence was based on the Totheroh interview and other research I had done, as well as carefully observing movement and weight of bodies, dust, foliage, and more at a variety of speeds until I felt I was seeing things at a "real life" adherence to the laws of gravity and physics.

picking the invisible mug up. This practice is then repeated for every segment of the overall action: you insert a pause after raising the mug to your mouth before taking a mimed sip, then another before removing it from your mouth, and once more when the mug is placed back on the table, and then again before removing your fingers from the mug handle. And so on.

Because without these little physical commas, you wind up with something of a blur of quick movements, and the audience can't quite tell what you are doing. Think of every "trapped in a box" mime bit you have seen, even the spoofs. Without that fraction-of-a-second beat of stillness after the performer places their flattened hand against the wall of the imaginary box, it just looks like the mime is waving at each of the nonexistent flat surfaces.

What I noticed and recognized in watching silent films at cranking speed were these same kinds of pauses. Not that the objects needed to be defined physically for the audience, since they were not being pantomimed, but so that the movement would not zip by and be harder to grasp or understand by the viewing audience. I don't think this was a deliberate application of mime skills by actors in silent film, but rather was a borrowed technique from performing in huge theaters or circuses that the performers were already used to.

Milton Sills references this technique in his article on motion picture acting as a required physical adjustment for the speed-up of silent film, although not in as much detail as I have:

> Another essential feature of the screen actor's technique is a careful spacing of significant items which constitute the sequence of the scene. One thing and one thing only must be done at a time, and this in a clean-cut and distinct style with no distracting, irrelevant or unnecessary movements.

If you watch a silent film at 66 or 75 percent of its projected speed, you will see these pauses. They are kind of like the pop-and-lock in breakdancing and hip-hop, where individual segments of a dance move have been broken up into several bits.

There is no name for this technique as far as I have been able to determine from the many conversations I have had with clowns and physical comedians over the last several years. Nor has it come out of the workshopping that happened during the silent-filmmaking experiments I have done with them. But they all understood instantly what I was talking about. I found that most of the time I did not need to explain much about this performance factor when we were filming our tests. Like what I had surmised about actors in motion pictures in the 1910s and 1920s, with these physical comedy performers it was already an understood and known component of their technique from years of live performance in front of audiences.

When we inserted these physical commas into actions, filmed them (digitally), and then watched the footage sped up by 35 to 50 percent, the pauses *disappeared*—and what we wound up with looked like silent film, just like the silent movies we have all seen, and not just film that is running faster.

I'm not sure exactly how this happens, but those pauses the performers insert so that "one thing and one thing only must be done at a time," as Sills describes...disappear. A magician will practice a move or a sequence of moves over and over until certain tiny bits of the motion they have rehearsed disappear and give the illusion of a single continuous movement.

This may also be related to the very principle upon which moving pictures are based. The pictures don't actually move, but through the persistence of vision, our brain combines the separate images together so that the pictures appear to be moving. The magician's sleight-of-hand techniques work the same way. The little pauses that give definition to bits of movement by separating them disappear in the speed-up of silent film.

Those pauses were part of what the performers in silent movies had baked into their muscle memory from days, weeks, months, years of touring and performing in theaters and circus tents. They had put in tens of the proverbial 10,000 hours making sure their movements read and were clear to everyone seated in the orchestra, mezzanine, and the nosebleed seats in the back of the second balcony.

Was this part of the "slow movement" Maurice Costello refers to? It may have been, or he or his many fellow performers may have reverted to this physicality out of habit. Remember my clown friend who said that the take that looked like a silent film felt to him like performing in a huge theater? It may have just naturally happened as actors and physical comedians saw or heard about what Costello—and, gradually, everyone else at Vitagraph—was doing.

We'll never know for sure. But what we do know is that there is a certain "look" that silent film performance has, from the early 1910s on, that you don't see when most people try making a silent film today. In addition to the adjusted performance tempo, there are those pauses, separating small beats of physical movement. And the same for reactions and facial expressions. The performances were still real and honest, and in the moment, but the thoughts or pieces of them were very slightly broken up.

The other kind of pause I have noticed that is used for definition is one that also accommodates the speed-up. It is one of repetition, usually when someone is pointing to something or at someone. The pointing is done two or three times. Only once, and it will blur by at a 30 to 50 percent fps increase. Repeated, it lands.

One thing I have enjoyed noticing while watching early talkies is that I can spot who had been in silents for only a couple years before the transition, and who had been in silents for ten to fifteen years. Because the actors who had been in silent pictures for a decade or so are still moving as if the cameras were turning at 16 or 18 fps. In *Sporting Blood*, a 1931 race-horse picture starring Clark Gable, Ernest Torrence (Keaton's father in *Steamboat Bill, Jr.*) performs, and delivers his lines, at a tempo that is around 30 percent slower than the actors he is in scenes with.

Character comedian Max Davidson does the same in his role as a mad scientist in the Harry Langdon talkie short *The Shrimp* (1930).

• • •

THE ALTERED REALITY OF
AN UNDERCRANKED WORLD

Buster Keaton said in interviews later in his life that one of the challenges of moving into feature-length films was that you couldn't do "impossible gags." I think he meant gags that weren't grounded in reality, that were borderline surreal, but that an audience watching silent film would accept without a need to question their feasibility or rationale.

Keaton was referring to gags that didn't have to be grounded in the story's reality—the surreal, bizarro gags that we associate with silent comedy shorts. Sure, he snuck a few in here and there—like the moment in *Seven Chances* (1925) when Keaton gets into his car, puts it in gear, and the *location* does a lap dissolve while Keaton and his auto remain immobile. He got away with it one last time by making almost all of *Sherlock, Jr.* (1924) a dream sequence. On the other hand, we expect these kinds of gags in silent movies, even when they continue into the second half of *Sherlock, Jr.* When dream Buster, the detective, dials the combination of a safe, opens its door, and exits out onto the street, as viewers we're not necessarily thinking, "Oh, of course, this is part of Buster's dream." In the Silent Film Universe this kind of gag could and did happen, often, in silent slapstick comedies. The kinds of gags and situations in the long dream fantasy sequence of

Sherlock, Jr. are so close to the kind that occur in silent comedy that when projectionist Buster ultimately wakes up, we have almost completely forgotten that we have been watching a dream at all.

This type of gag, which Keaton referred to as "impossible," brings us back to what I noticed about Chaplin in the employment office in *A Dog's Life*. With silent film, as a gag writer or stunt coordinator, you had the freedom to create gags and stunts that can't happen in real life because reality grounds you with the laws of physics and gravity.

Silent film's ubiquitous undercranking, aided by its silence and monochromic unreality, allowed creators in the 1910s and 1920s to think and create the way cartoon gag writers and directors did in the 1930s and, especially, in the 1940s.

What is clear to me from watching hundreds of silent comedies, as well as westerns, serials, and action pictures like those of Douglas Fairbanks, is that everyone understood you could come up with a gag, stunt, or piece of business that could not be done in real life. And, by reverse engineering it through choreography and/or adjusted movement, combined with a specific cranking speed and perhaps elements of stagecraft and sleight-of-hand, that gag or stunt could be made to exist.

The expectation of reality with silent film is such that, as a creator, you don't have to have much regard for logic, consequence, or laws of physics. The audience will pretty much buy anything it sees on the screen, because the Silent Film Universe is on another plane of reality from the one we experience outside of silent film.

That reality does not exist in sound film. When talking pictures came to be the norm in 1929–1930, the people working in motion pictures were not just adding talk. Their work as creators and artists could no longer reside in the Silent Film Universe. This is what comedians and action performers lost when sound came in. The paired real-time speed of the camera and recorded sound now grounded the actors' performances, scenes, and stories much more closely to reality. It went much deeper than "we had to tell jokes now" or that Chaplin now had to consider finding a voice for the Little Tramp.

In silent film, you had—and still have—free rein to come up with absolutely anything you could imagine and put it on the screen, especially if it was something you could only conceive of happening in a dream. The dream-like state of watching silent movies could not and cannot happen, or happen the same way, with sound film.

The unique form of silent film allowed the performers, directors, scenarists, gag writers, and stunt performers to unleash their imaginations. The medium became for them a jumping-off point into what turned out to be the Silent Film Universe, and not an end point or culmination of their days, weeks, and years of performing and creating for a live audience.

• • •

What is both fascinating and baffling is how this realization happened among the entire population of people working in moving pictures, both in front of and behind the camera, and how it spread throughout the silent filmmaking community. From watching films of the 1910s, the shift appears to have happened somewhere during the years 1913 to 1916. This is when Keystone, established in 1912, really hit its stride stylistically and when the popularity of serials really took hold. Yes, not all Keystone shorts were wildly physical and not all serials were full of chases. But in both cases, as well as with the comedies made by L-KO[18] and eventually even at Vita-graph, there is a stretching of the limits of reality.

It's hard to imagine that there were people sitting around talking about film theory like they were cinema studies students in the 1960s or 1970s, musing about the notions I have been outlining as far as elements being left out and then filled in by the audience's imaginations. But something clearly happened, and developed, within a few years' time: the understanding that you could pretty much get away with anything, without explaining it or having to justify it by showing the main character eating Welsh rare-bit and then falling asleep.

Physical comedians and stunt performers may have stumbled onto some of these techniques by happy acci-dent, noticing something while watching rushes the day after filming. Maybe they caught a movie in a theater on its last show of the day, when the projectionist was over-speeding the film because it was late and he wanted to go home, and they saw some action onscreen that had been one way on set and suddenly became something else

---

[18] L-KO was Lehrman-Knockout Comedies, founded by Keystone director Henry "Pathé" Lehrman in 1914. L-KO shorts were released through Uni-versal until the company ceased production in 1919.

when sped up. Perhaps those performers realized they could take the idea they saw even further and tried it in a scene they were taking the next day, reverse engineering some piece of business so it would work differently when projected faster.

This is similar to the moment in silent cinema, although a gradual one, when the title that announced what was about to transpire stopped being used. How did this happen? Who thought, "Well, this is overkill," and wrote

Back view of a Pathé Frères motion picture camera. This camera was used by a majority of cinematographers in the 1900s and 1910s. Note that its only dial indicates footage count and not cranking rate.
(photo by Dino Everett; camera is from the collection of the USC HMH Foundation Moving Image Archive)

a title that poetically introduced the scene instead…and found that audiences weren't confused?

I have to imagine that many people in the motion picture business were trying out what Maurice Costello said he did once he came upon the idea of moving a little slower. He tried out the movement adjustments in a film he was making and then, when he saw in a theater, it worked.

Every week, there was so much film being made and released and viewed and reflected upon that there was room for this kind of trial-and-error experimentation with physical movement. When it succeeded, you could then play with how far the technique could be taken. The same could be tried with leaving out bits of action when cutting from one shot to the next, as could the discovery of optimal cranking speeds for different kinds of action.

Who figured out that you could show someone dive *head-first* out a window, and then in the next shot land on their *feet* outdoors, and that it would look like one continuous movement, one so quick that no one noticed the continuity mistake? Somebody gave it a whirl and found out the illusion worked when the shots were cut together and projected at a faster-than-filmed-at speed.

What I have seen develop in films of the 1920s takes this creative experimentation even further. The poetry-like elisions of elements or showing just enough of a key dramatic element or beat continues to develop. In comedies, many gags are created where what is going to wind up on the screen cannot exist in reality and is not a gag in real time, but can become one if staged a certain way, and cranked at a specific speed. In the frenetic comedies of Larry Semon, there is often a shot during a high-speed chase when people are running down a street—with the camera following alongside in a car—where it looks like Larry's and his pursuers' legs are not moving. It's similar to something you may have seen in movies where the spokes on a tire in motion do not appear to be moving. This only had to happen once during the filming of a chase that was viewed later. The cameraman[19] then figured out that this effect could be achieved again, as long as the performers ran at the same speed as before and the camera did as well.

The "step right up and call me Speedy" jig in Harold Lloyd's *The Freshman* (1925) cannot be executed in real life the way it appears onscreen. And yet, when viewed at what I am estimating was cranking speed for the takes with the jig, the steps Lloyd takes are very simple, and the jig is not funny. Until it is projected at 24 fps (or faster).

The more I looked at silent film sequences at their cranking speeds, the more I saw the reverse engineering of the physical actions, from dramatic scenes to wild slapstick. And, clearly, everyone was in on it.

What is really intriguing is how little they spoke about it in interviews, both during the silent era and even when being interviewed by Kevin Brownlow for his book *The Parade's Gone By* (1968, University of California Press) or his legendary documentary series *Hollywood* (1980).

• • •

[19] Semon's cameraman was usually Hans Koenekamp.

A brief P.S. to my observations about cranking speeds—and that is about the use of "overcranking" or slow motion. I have seen this used in two ways.

One is to indicate or emulate inadvertent drunkenness. A child, dog, or horse (or a pig, as in Murnau's *Sunrise*) has accidentally lapped up alcohol, and then we cut to slow-motion footage of the person or animal moving about. I get this…how else can you get a dog or a child to simulate tipsy behavior? The same technique is used with adults when they have inhaled ether, as in the climax of the battle between bootleggers and revenue men[20] in *Feel My Pulse* (1928) starring Bebe Daniels and William Powell.

The other place I have seen overcranking used is in over-head shots of someone diving into the ocean—usually a bathing beauty—but only in overhead shots. Dives photographed straight-on are usually taken at the usual frame rate.

•　•　•

PROJECTION SPEED AND SILENT FILM

Everyone has an opinion about what speed silent films should be shown at, and what the "correct" speed is for silent film. A lot of the time it is subjective. Often, those subjective opinions match the history of projection speeds during the silent era. Sometimes they don't.

There are a lot of terms that get used and thrown about when this is discussed: silent speed, sound speed, too fast, too slow, "natural motion," that line about the Keystone Kops.

---

[20] Government agents whose task it was during Prohibition (1920–1933) to catch and arrest anyone illegally making alcohol.

What I have found in my research is that there was not one, single frames-per-second, feet-per-minute, minutes-per-reel projection speed for silent movies. It changed, gradually, throughout the silent era.

What is often referred to as "silent speed," which hovers in the territory of 16 to 18 frames per second, was a speed that motion pictures were shown at in theaters up through the early or mid-1910s. Most of the time.

A basic all-use speed could be recommended, but there was no way to enforce an intended or standardized one. Initially, all projectors were hand-cranked, which meant that one mandated speed could not be locked in on all machines manufactured. Even after motors were added to projectors in the mid-1910s, trade publications do not show evidence of an effort to mechanically implement a specific uniform speed for all motion pictures. There are articles and even film reviews encouraging a specific speed as a norm. Occasionally, a report or editorial by the trade paper's appointed expert on the subject will mention a projectionist at a theater they have visited who prided themself on keeping their hand on the motor's rheostat speed control and adjusting a film scene by scene.

However, projectionists simply ran the film at a chosen rate because it eliminated flicker and the risk of fire, and/or because it was set by the theater manager to be faster than a speed prescribed by the distributor in order to fit their cinema's schedule. This was done to accommodate the number of shows per day. Sometimes it was just a matter of the projectionist wanting to go home a little early at the end of the day. A projection speed was not standardized and locked in until it had to be, when synchronized sound was added to movies.

As Maurice Costello discovered when he began acting in moving pictures in 1908, films might be shown at an even faster rate than the 16 or 18 fps mentioned above. Not every reel was exactly 1,000 feet of film, and even once feature length took hold in the mid-1910s, most of these films were five or six reels—but not all. Occasionally, they were seven or even eight reels in length. Exhibitors needed to be able to guarantee they would have a certain number of shows per day, for ticket sales that would help cover film rentals. Trade magazines like the *Moving Picture World* have articles starting in 1915 about exhibitors wanting to standardize their shows' start times so moviegoers would know when to show up. This was less of an issue in the earlier days of programs of a handful of single-reel films that ran throughout the day and evening.

So, to fit a certain number of shows in on a given day, one might have to run a picture faster. You can't have the same number of shows in a day with a two-reel Lonesome Luke comedy and a six-reel drama as you can with a one-reel Joker comedy and a five-reel drama.

What I am still looking for documentation on—factually or in editorials—is something I have to assume happened for economic reasons. You can't expect an exhibitor to run the films slower and have one fewer show per day and sell one fewer audience's worth of tickets, and you can't tell the production companies to crank faster to try and catch up, thereby spending more money on motion picture film. And so, at a point I have observed as happening in the early 1910s, this discrepancy between filming and projection speeds just stuck.

What I have found, interestingly, is a gradual increase of projection speeds during the silent era, from the early 1910s through the late 1920s. This has come from research I have done going through trade publications, and from my four decades of accompanying silent films.

Stanley Watkins, an engineer at Western Electric, essentially set the frame rate for "sound speed," and in a 1961 an interview talks about how this was decided. Watkins said that the projection speed chosen for talking pictures—90 feet per minute, or 24 fps—did not come from months of exhaustive research.

What was done, Watkins stated, is that they asked the head of Warner Bros theaters what speed(s) the films were being shown at around the country. They were told the biggest houses in the big cities were using 80 feet a minute (21–22 fps) and the smaller houses were going at 100 feet a minute (27 fps) or faster (!), usually depending on how many shows they needed to get in every day.[21]

And so, in setting a standard speed for talking pictures, the decision was made to split the difference, and sound speed was set at 90 feet per minute, or 24 fps.

• • •

As much as one may watch silent films of the 1920s and feel like they are being run too fast, it's important to be

---

[21] *The Speed of Sound* by Scott Eyman (Simon & Schuster, 1997).

aware of what was actually happening in theaters at the time. Keep in mind also that cameramen were aware of the speeds at which their films were being shown, as were the directors and performers.

Earl Sponable was the technical director of Fox-Case Corporation in New York; he and Theodore Case were key developers of the Movietone sound-on-film system. In September 1927, Sponable gave a talk at a meeting of the Society of Motion Picture Engineers which was then published as "Some Technical Aspects of the Movietone" in the SMPE's journal.

Sponable's talk is mostly about recording and sound reproduction and the finer points of the Movietone sound-on-film system for talking pictures. At one point, his address veers into the subject of running speeds. Sponable addresses a question about how oil on the film affects sound reproduction and references the Society's arriving at a standard speed of 90 feet per minute for talkies, after there had been some back and forth between using 85 or 90.

What he says next is fascinating:

> In connection with the Society's standard, I have been unable to find any New York theater which is running film at 85 feet a minute; the present normal speed is *105 feet* [italics mine], and on Sundays often 120 feet per minute is used in order to get in an extra show.

105 feet per minute is 28 frames per second. So...people were seeing films at 28 fps in many theaters by 1927. And sometimes at 32 fps on Sundays.

•   •   •

In my experience of creating and performing live accompaniment to silent films over many years, I have developed a sixth sense, one that is sort of an internal governor or gauge about film projection speeds. I have found that I and my fellow film accompanists all have developed a sense of projection speed that is "in the pocket," or "just right." Not just from how the film looks, but from what we do in support of it and how it feels in doing so.

Accompanying films being run a bit slower than they ought to be is more work. There is a certain amount of drama and forward energy that has to be supplied musically on top of the usual amount of emotional boosting (where needed) in the accompaniment of a silent film.

Silent era cinematographer Arthur Reeves with his Bell & Howell 2709 motion picture camera (ca. 1920s). The 2709 was in heavy use at most studios in the 1910s and 1920s.
(photo courtesy of the USC HMH Foundation Moving Image Archive)

Similarly, there is more effort to be put in by the accompanist with over-speeding because this too-fast state can mask or lessen the characters' emotional states or decision-making, and the same can happen with essential bits of movements. The films become slightly harder to decode visually, and as accompanists we need to find ways to help the audience connect emotionally with dramatic moments that the over-speeding now glosses over.

I'll tell you what my rule of thumb is, and you are free to disagree with it or to adopt a "your mileage may vary" outlook on it. (Keep in mind that my thumb-rule below is for American-made silent films; during the 1920s, in France the average projection speed was below 24 fps and in Germany it was above 24, often closer to 30 fps.)

Side view of the Bell & Howell 2709. As with the Pathé Frères, the camera's dials only indicate footage count and not cranking rate.
(photo by Dino Everett; camera is from the collection of the USC HMH Foundation Moving Image Archive)

141

The numbers below refer to frames per second:

- early 1910s—pretty much across the board, 16–18; comedies (especially slapstick) by 1913 or 1914…18–20 (comedies seem to always have been run faster than dramas)

- mid-1910s—18 for dramas, and 20 for comedies

- late teens to early 1920s—18–20 for dramas, and 20–22 for comedies

- early 1920s—some comedy shorts may run fine at 24; I've seen press sheets for a number of two-reel comedies from the early 1920s that indicate a total footage of 2,000 feet and a running time of 22 minutes (that's 24 fps)

- starting in 1923—and I don't know why this seems to kick in in 1923—most silent films, including dramatic features, play well at 24 and were shown at this speed

- late 1920s—24 to 27

This set of projection rates comes from my knowledge and understanding of what speed the films were shown at in theaters, and the fact that the people making films were aware of this and compensated for the anticipated speed-up. They did so in cutting rhythms, in physical movement, and in cranking speeds used (no film was taken at just one consistent frame rate for every shot in a film). I have endeavored to empathically understand all this from the perspective of what was going through the minds of people who made the films, as opposed to just objectively gauging silent films' projection speed from how a film looks to me.

These are my observations and experiences with silent film projection speeds. There are nuances and shadings I may have left out or overlooked. But I hope this provides food for thought in understanding not only what an appropriate speed for projecting a particular silent film may be, but also understanding why you may feel like a silent you are watching seems like it is running too slow or too fast.

•   •   •

THE MYTH/MISNOMER OF "SILENT SPEED"

Let's take a moment to consider the term "silent speed" as a way people in the sound era (and even today) define the projected frames-per-second rate for silent movies.

There is a notion that silent films should be shown at what is often referred to as "silent speed," or 18 fps. It is a term accepted and used by film programmers, historians, projectionists, people supervising film transfers, and technicians or editors implementing speed adjustment to digital files.

As discussed above, projection speeds may have started off in the 1900s and the early 1910s as being 16–18 fps, but typical running speeds crept up to 24 fps by the early to mid-1920s, and faster by the late 1920s. So, then, where does the concept of the term "silent speed," meaning a projection rate of 16 fps or 18 fps for silent movies, come from?

My hunch is that all this has to do with home movies.

In 1923, 16mm safety film was introduced to the consumer market as a home movie format by Eastman Kodak. Just two years later, the company launched the Kodascope Library to rent films—ones that had been shown in theaters—to the home movie enthusiast on 16mm safety film. In 1925, Universal launched its "Show-At-Home Library," and a handful of other film rental libraries followed suit. If you figure the time it must have taken to get studio permission, get 35mm prints to reduce to 16mm, design and build equipment to make these rental prints, go through trial-and-error with the use of camphor oil treatments for the prints,[22] build the libraries and delivery system, create the catalogs, and so forth, the idea of showing movies screened in theaters in your own home must have been part of the plan all along.

Let us now consider the projectors made and sold to the 16mm home movie enthusiast in the 1920s.

The movie cameras ran at 16 fps. This speed was chosen because it would give the home movie maker the maximum running time on a 100-foot roll of 16mm—a little over three minutes—without having a noticeable flicker when projected.

The 16mm home movie projectors sold in the 1920s either ran at 16 fps or, more commonly, had a rheostat that would start at 16 fps and go up from there.

Why?

[22] Camphor oil was used as a preservative and was used by the Kodascope Library to treat the films so they would hold up under multiple uses. If you find a 16mm film that smells like mothballs, chances are it is a Kodascope print.

My guess is that the intention was not to give home movie makers the opportunity to make their home movies look silly, but instead that they would be able to run rented 16mm prints of studio product at a speed akin to how they were run in theaters.

Surviving Kodascope rental catalogs do not contain instructions for running speeds, nor do instruction manuals for 1920s home movie projectors indicate the purpose of the projector motor's rheostat.

In the 1930s, 16mm projectors with optical sound capability hit the market. Sound cartoons and comedy shorts, and eventually features, were added to the rental libraries.

I have seen 16mm projectors from the 1940s and onward that have a speed switch on them. The projectors needed to be able to run at 24 fps to show the 16mm optical sound prints that were available from camera shops and rental libraries. If you were also a home movie maker, you needed to be able to show your home movies, which run at 16 fps.

These projectors have switches on them labeled:

"SILENT / SOUND"

The "silent" option was intended for home movies, which were double-perforated 16mm and were mute, and the "sound" option was for the library-loaned/rented prints, which had optical soundtracks. The "silent" setting ran the projector at 16 fps and the "sound" setting at 24 fps.

These 16mm optical sound projectors did not have motor speed rheostats, just that either/or switch. Silent films were still being rented, but the medium was relegated to antique status in the industry and popular culture. If you were showing rented or borrowed studio-product movies to your friends in 16mm, you would certainly be aiming to present sound films. This silent/sound switch on 16mm projectors persisted for decades, and they were on the Bell & Howell and Kodak Pageant machines I used in middle and high school.

What I surmise from this is that is the origin of the term "silent speed" stems from several decades of uses of 16mm projectors that had silent/sound switches on them—intended for showing home movies as opposed to studio or educational films in homes, schools, auditoriums, and elsewhere. I believe that this conflated idea led to the assumption that all silent movies should be shown at a frame rate of 16 or 18 fps, a speed that was established and set for *home movies*. "Silent speed" meant your family or amateur films would be projected at the same speed at which they were filmed, yielding "natural movement."

•　　•　　•

The term "natural motion" is a phrase I have heard invoked when a projection speed has been selected that is slower than the one at which the film was originally shown. It is occasionally followed or backed up by that "Keystone Kops" adage.

The thing is, "natural motion" is not really achievable. That is, unless you are showing home movies, actualities from the turn of the last century, or maybe newsreel footage.

Running silent film at cranking speed or close to it ends up looking a bit slow-motion. True, you are seeing the performers at real-time speed—how it looked on the shooting stages when the cameras were turning. But the reason a silent film feels "too slow" to people who sense that the slower projection speed is a bit off—despite the claims of aiming for "natural motion"—is that the actors have adjusted their movement and physicality to compensate for the expected-in-cinemas speed-up. And that is what we are now witnessing with the film running at "silent speed," seeing the film at or near cranking speed. This movement adjusting is borne out by the statements we have from Maurice Costello and Milton Sills.

What actors were doing in adopting "a deliberate tempo" in performing for an undercranked camera, as Sills referred to it, was done on purpose in order to achieve the simulation or replication of natural motion for when the films were projected at a faster rate in cinemas. Projection at cranking speed reveals the physical compensation and is not the way people naturally move. But the projected, faster speed yields the *intended* physical tempos of real time, the illusion which the actors were aiming for.

This is because the performers had control over their physical movements. However, when it comes to elements of nature—wind, water, and gravity—this adjustment was impossible to accommodate.

I became aware of this while exploring a facet of the way filming speeds can be used in the Silent Film Universe.

Silent film, because it is projected faster than its taking speed, allowed (and allows) for the mixing of cranking speeds. Since it is all running faster than real life, you can cut from a shot taken at 12 to another at 16 to another at 8, and back. Most of Keaton's *One Week* (1920) is taken at one speed—most probably 16 fps, which I have ascertained from slowing the footage down to what resembles reality, and then noting the percentage of the speed reduction. But when I examined the wide shot of the house spinning—utilizing this same slowdown procedure and math—I found it looked like it was filmed at around 8 fps. My gauge for how far to slow this shot down was by looking at the trees blowing in the wind and rain in the shot. I have also noticed that during the house-spinning sequence the house appears to be turning at different rates in different shots, because those were filmed at different speeds.

But, regardless of the taking speed, a deliberate tempo cannot be applied to people running, or to the law of gravity.

You cannot adjust the speed you are running to compensate for the speed-up, because when you run slower you are no longer *running*. You cannot get a horse to run slower, because that gallop just becomes a trot or canter. Sped-up footage of people or animals running just looks frenetic, no matter what you do.

And gravity is gravity. People and things fall at the speed at which they naturally fall.

What I have noticed in silent movies, over many years, is that the shots of people running about and of objects

large and small falling were never taken at a faster cranking speed to compensate for the velocity at which people
move or at which objects plummet. When I was working
on the home video edition of the restored Marion Davies
silent feature *When Knighthood Was in Flower* (1922)—released by my label Undercrank Productions in 2017—I
found that while most of the film looks "fine" at one
speed, the entirety of the film's climax, with knights chasing each other on horseback, looks faster than the rest of
the film does.

You could certainly make the case for adjusting the
playback speed of those scenes to even things out for the
Blu-ray/DVD edition. But I also figured…it's 1922, and
by this point the camera operators knew what people
chasing each other around on horse and on foot looked
like, and if they wanted it to be in line with the rest of the
picture, they would have cranked these scenes at 20–22
fps so the movement matched the rest of the film.

But they didn't. And this is not the only film where
I have seen this. It's not that uncommon in silent film,
actually.

The closest thing to "natural motion" in projecting
silent film is to run the film at the speed it was shown at
during its release, to honor the work put into what we are
seeing by the performers and other artisans who worked
so hard on these movies decades ago. Because the people
who made the films were aiming to achieve—in moving
at a deliberate tempo for film that would be shown a bit
faster, later—a different plane of "natural motion," one
that only exists in the Silent Film Universe.

• • •

ACCESSIBLE TO ALL PEOPLE OF ALL ERAS

I believe that what I am referring to as undercranking as it pertains to silent film is an essential part of the core of why silent film still works and is easily accessible for a contemporary audience of all ages. Silent film is a trifecta of silence, monochrome, and, especially, this speed-up of film that does not appear over-sped. This unique blending of cinematic elements is the backbone of what silent cinema could do and what allows for the Silent Film Universe to exist.

Film that is merely sped up, without the physical compensation, does not have the same effect.

The innate effect of silent film undercranking—the chosen and precise slower cranking and physical movement intended for slightly faster projection—in conjunction with the silence and the monochrome imagery enables the existence of an enhanced, otherworldly reality. Processed by the right brain along with all the other elements of silent film, it allows the viewer's imagination and bond with the film to go further, and it meant the same for people creating and making movies during the silent era. It's the reason we can be presented with the otherworldliness of silent film and can quite easily accept pretty much anything that is put on screen as the film's reality. It allows us as viewers up and into the Silent Film Universe, that near-dreamlike world of silent movies that we enjoy so much.

This is what came crashing to earth with talking pictures. Because once reality is being photographed and played back in real time, and audiences are grounded further by being able to hear dialogue and ambient sound, our expectation of reality must be honored, and not played with.

We will never know why no one involved in making moving pictures in the 1910s and 1920s ever talked about the speed-up and how it was compensated for and deliberately utilized. Perhaps the practice was so matter-of-fact and commonplace that no one being interviewed about their work, during or after the silent era, thought of it as special and worth noting to make sure everyone knew about it. Perhaps it was because of the ridicule silents received almost immediately when talking pictures arrived and took over.

But from everything I have observed, researched, and played with in trying to replicate the effect, I have to believe this technique was an essential part of the filmmaking language in silent film. Because the performances read just fine and are as easily decoded when the film is run faster, we have never noticed it. Deconstructing sequences and shots from silent films and dissecting the process has been revelatory for me—and confirms this.

From the antics of 1912–1915 Keystone comedies up through the visual-storytelling poetry of late silents like *The Crowd* (1928) and everything in between—Keaton's and Pickford's and Fairbanks's films, Soviet cinema, German Expressionism, and on and on—audiences of the time and of today are lifted up into the Silent Film Universe. Regardless of being part of a particular culture or era, silent film still works.

10.

SILENT FILM AFTER THE SILENT ERA

Filmmakers' love for silent cinema has held on throughout the post-1929 decades. The form has popped up in movies from time to time either as blueprint or as inspiration—sometimes both.

What I am referring to here are endeavors to make new silent movies, either as films that attempt to replicate the form of silent cinema or films that use little to no dialog. These are the films people will tell me about because they know of my deep interest in and passion for silent movies. They will ask me what I think about *Blancanieves* (2012), *Sidewalk Stories* (1989), films by director Guy Maddin, or the television program *Mr. Bean* (1990–1995). And then there are the films with reduced amounts of dialog like John Krasinski's *A Quiet Place* (2018) or a picture like *All Is Lost* (2013) with Robert Redford, in which Redford has almost no dialog.

There have been films made that are loving tributes to silent cinema like Carl Reiner's *The Comic* (1969) or Blake Edwards's *The Great Race* (1965), and attempts at replicating the medium itself like Michel Hazanavicius's *The Artist* (2011). The wordless or reduced-dialogue sync-sound films are worth discussing here, for the sake of inclusion, since the artists who made these were heavily influenced by filmmakers and performances from the silent era.

Over the past several decades, new silent movies have been made in a way that deliberately resembles their pre-1930 counterparts. While some of these new silents have met with critical or popular success, they have all been one-offs and have not spawned any sort of resurgence of the medium of silent film or silent filmmaking. In adopting the format of silent cinema, some of these sound-era efforts have been more successful than others at aesthetically adopting or utilizing the medium.

I am distinguishing between "format" and "medium," because not all of the aspects of silent film I have been discussing are always in evidence in the sound era silents that have been made. Sometimes this is deliberate on the part of the filmmakers; sometimes this is inadvertent. Until now, what filmmakers knew of the cinematic language of silent movies may have been based on an unintentionally limited or conflated (mis)understanding of the medium, merely following stereotypes perpetuated in spoofs made in the first decade of the sound era. On the other end of the spectrum, some of these filmmakers may have done a good deal of research and film viewing in an effort to evoke the visual and pantomimic traditions of silent movies' storytelling.

In all of these cases, the playing with the audience's or viewers' expectations of reality and invitation into a more right-brained screen experience is at the core, whether it was consciously intended by the filmmakers or not.

• • •

Movie stars of the 1920s did the best they could to hang on to aspects of the mute cinematic form they had been entrenched in, and in some cases helped develop, thus far. The talkie transition was a sea change in a variety of ways for people who had been in silents for several years or longer. The top starring comedians of silent movies were the last to give up the ghost when talking pictures brought the Silent Film Universe back down to earth. I can't say I blame them. Physical and visual comedy was what they were known for, and they weren't joke comics, really. They could be, but so could every other comedian under contract to any given studio.

Stars of dramatic films pivoted right away and managed to adapt and continue onward. Many left the moving picture business after a few years. The movie-making game had changed, and the atmosphere on the shooting stages—now called sound stages—was very different. You had to be quiet on the set, memorize lines, and learn blocking that was dictated by both the dramatic action and the placement of a microphone. The on-set mood music, while-the-cameras-were-turning verbal coaching from the director, and ever-present purring of the cameras were all gone now.

The stars of action movies did not have an easy time of it. Douglas Fairbanks, Sr. gave it his best shot, having come from the theater and been a star on Broadway for several years before entering movies. But action pictures as they were, and could be, in the silent era would take some years to reconfigure to suit the new medium. After his last silent film in 1929, western superstar Tom Mix returned to the circus—where he had cut his teeth before entering motion pictures in 1909—for a few years before making movies again.

The star comedians found ways to keep their physical comedy craft in use, in varying degrees, depending on which studio they were working for and how sympathetic their creative teams were to setting talk aside here and there for physical business.

Keaton did what he could in the films he made for the MGM studio system, adding falls, business, or other sight gags where there were opportunities. Lloyd rolled up his sleeves and did his best to carry the traditions of his screen character and of physical comedy into what comedy films were becoming in the early 1930s. Harry Langdon made shorts at Hal Roach, where his creative team did their best to adapt Harry's screen character to two-reel talking comedies, with this adaptation continuing through shorts for Educational Pictures, where he (thankfully) talked less while doing comedy business.

Laurel & Hardy had already been slowing their pacing down, so when the reality of real-time speed and sync sound let the helium out of the balloon for silent era comedians, Stan and Babe were already set. One of their last silent shorts, *Wrong Again* (1929)—one of my favorites—has slapstick sequences, but it also has an unusual segment about seven minutes in. Having delivered a racehorse to its rightful owner—as far as Stan and Ollie understood the situation—they sit on a couch and have a conversation about the oddness of this, aided by a handful of simple dialog title cards. For a minute and a half. In a silent film.

Chaplin, of course, was *Chaplin* and didn't have to give up the medium if he didn't want to. He didn't, and he made two more silent films after the advent of talkies. There are so many gags and routines in *City Lights* (1931) that could never happen or work in a sound film, that are only able to exist in the Silent Film Universe, it's almost as if he was shouting, "Look what you're giving up!" I'm sure that wasn't his intention in creating the iconic boxing match and other sequences, but in *City Lights* Chaplin continues building on the feature-length silent cinematic progression he had been on with *The Gold Rush* (1925) and *The Circus* (1928).

This continues with his last silent film, *Modern Times* (1936), which he interestingly used to make a statement about modern times and which he set—notably—in modern times. No one is dressed like it is the 1910s or 1920s. No one drives older cars or anything like that. The society we see in the film and its storyline is that of the mid-1930s. The automobiles we see are 1935–36 automobiles. The men and women we see wear mid-1930s clothing and hats.

At some point in the late 1930s, though, screwball and other dialog-driven comedies moved physical and slapstick comedy to a sort of "class clown" designation outside of the mainstream. Silent era comedians Buster Keaton, Harry Langdon, and Charley Chase were making shorts at Columbia Pictures, working under Jules White and on lower-budget and lower-brow conditions. Laurel & Hardy were winding down their best work, and only in feature-length films. Lloyd basically retired from the screen, and Chaplin made his first "talkie," *The Great Dictator* (1940). The other comedians, such as Hank Mann or Snub Pollard, pop up in bit parts in features, continuing to work and to pay their bills.

But again—with the exception of Chaplin prior to his making *The Great Dictator* —these folks are not making silent films, as I have defined the medium. These comedians are doing nonverbal sight gags and physical business in the realm of the talking comedies they are in. They are making sound movies with silent bits or routines in them. Silent film is over and left behind, and it was subjected to ridicule by the public, the critics, and the industry as a cinematic and cultural antique.

It would not be until two decades after the "talkie" transition that nonverbal and physical comedy would return to the screen in any sort of important way.

• • •

It came from France.

Ironically, similar to the way Sennett was influenced by the physical comedy shorts made around 1907–1913 by Gaumont and Eclipse in France, and by Ambrosio in Italy—released both in Europe and in the USA—the next big influence for screen comedy made its way to American shores in the 1950s. Perhaps because the history and tradition of physical comedy performance ran deeper in France, the success of Jacques Tati's short films made there in the 1940s led to his move into features. These were released not only in Europe but also in the USA and were successful on both continents.

To my mind, without Tati's *Monsieur Hulot's Holiday* (1953) and *Mon Oncle* (1958)—and possibly his 1949 *Jour de Fête*, depending on how widely seen it may have been in the USA—there is no Jerry Lewis in *The Bellboy* (1960)

The Bellboy (1960), starring and directed by Jerry Lewis, whose character and comedy business are without dialog while inhabiting a "sound film" reality—until the very end of the film. (courtesy of Jerry Lewis)

or *The Ladies Man* (1961) or *The Errand Boy* (1961); no Ernie Kovacs in *Eugene* (half-hour TV specials in 1957 and 1961, and an unrealized feature film), nor Blake Edwards's *The Party* (1968), or Rowan Atkinson's *Mr. Bean*. There may not have been a direct, conscious dot-connecting on the part of Mr. Lewis and Mr. Kovacs, but Stanley the bellhop at the Fontainebleau Hotel and Eugene the fish-out-of-water at a stodgy private men's club follow the same "you can do this without a traditional narrative" model as Monsieur Hulot's summer at the Hotel de la Plage or his friendship with his city-dwelling nephew.

Tati, Lewis, and Kovacs share with their silent era counterparts their being leading character comedians who are also filmmakers. (Kovacs never got to make movies of his own, but many of the sketches on his television shows were shot and cut live in the control room in a way that resembles cinema.) I have noticed that the existence of the silent comedian or star comedian doubling as cinema auteur is a phenomenon that the silent era seems to have, remarkably, lent itself to. There were more comedians directing themselves in their films during the 1920s than there ever were in the years that followed.

Both Jerry Lewis and Ernie Kovacs were comedian/auteurs who had an interest in visual and physical comedy as it applies to screen entertainment. Watching their long-form TV comedy sketches tells us they both instinctively knew there was something else you could do in feature films than the standard Hollywood studio stuff, where a comedian would be plugged into one of a number of typical plots. Director Blake Edwards had a similar interest in physical and visual humor, and once he combined creative forces with Peter Sellers you had another unreliant-on-dialog comedian-filmmaker, although in this case it was spread across two creative forces.

•   •   •

There is a lot of power and expression in leaving dialog out of a sync-sound film, for the whole film or for segments of it. There is an element of vulnerability and innocence in a mute or nonverbal character who is immersed in a community of talking people. For an audience, a character's communicating without speaking or our being informed by his or her nonverbal performance draws us in. It is that right-brain factor that is such a core element of silent film, inviting us to fill in or imagine the thought processes of those characters. This is where a parallel to silent film occurs, although what is more easily noticeable to most people is just the fact that these characters are silent. In comedy films of the 1950s and 1960s that have a nonspeaking character, the otherworldliness of silent film is aimed at via the employing of a nonlinear narrative, one that is occasionally helped along by creative or clever uses of sound.

A nonspeaking character, or one who doesn't speak in some sequences of a film or television program, is also an island for us in the audience—a break from all the talk and the left-brain-only proceedings. In Marx Brothers films, Harpo perfectly balances the verbal antics and sparring of Groucho and Chico for us.

Wordless characters have a long tradition going back decades and generations in theater, mime, circus, vaudeville and music hall, commedia dell'arte, and the like. Perhaps this is why Jacques Tati was emboldened enough to expand this speech-less comedic tradition into feature films in the post-silent era. The same could be said for anyone in the financing or production end of Tati's first couple of features who said "yes" to a film that is nothing more than following an efficiency-driven postman delivering the mail or Mr. Hulot simply vacationing—with neither of them caught up in high stakes dramatic storylines such as getting involved in a romance or in trouble with gangsters. Tati's films featuring a main character who does not speak were very successful, in Europe and in the USA, and the blueprint set by his format can be seen in other films that have followed, from Jackie Gleason's *Gigot* (1962) to Rowan Atkinson's *Mr. Bean's Holiday* (2007).

The Ernie Kovacs Special – *"Eugene"* (1961), starring and directed by Ernie Kovacs. Kovacs's mute character exists in an altered reality of bizarre sight gags, incongruous sounds, and—as seen here—gravity that has gone askew. (courtesy of Ediad Productions, Inc.)

Comedians who had physical comedy performance in their bones or had an affinity for it and worked in television in the 1950s and 1960s found opportunities to do "silent" or pantomime sketches, such as Red Skelton, Lucille Ball, Jackie Gleason, and, possibly with more invention to it, the aforementioned Jerry Lewis and Ernie Kovacs. You had to have the confidence to not talk for a few minutes or more on television, which was a rare condition. Ernie Kovacs went so far as to make humorous, wordless 90-second TV commercials for his sponsor Dutch Masters cigars during 1959–1961.

There are many instances that could be cited here where the absence of dialog has been flirted with—for example, Ray Milland in *The Thief* (1952), John Krasinski's *A Quiet Place* franchise, or episodes of various sitcoms where the main character takes a vow of silence or has laryngitis. Although any of these have an absence of or do not rely on dialog, and one could refer to these characters, scenes, or films as being "silent," they are not *silent films*. They exist in the filmed-at-projection-speed, sync-sound, and (usually) full-color world that is a few simple steps removed from reality yet not quite enough steps to inhabit the Silent Film Universe.

• • •

A handful of filmmakers have tried their hand at capturing the magic of silent film. Their new silent movies received good reviews and did well at the box office. Reviewers and fans wondered, each time, if this might be signaling a resurgence of interest in silent movies and the making of silents.

It didn't.

Over the two years that followed the release of *The Artist* (2011), during my show intros or Q and As I would ask the audience how many people were at the show because they had seen *The Artist* and now wanted to see more silent films.

Zero hands went up. Every time.

Hmm. That's weird. We all thought that this film really resembled the silent movies we love, and it did well at the box office. Many people who had never been to a silent movie went to see *The Artist*. The film won Oscars, BAFTAs, and other awards. This sure looked like it would be the thing that would finally win over our friends who we could not drag to go see a Buster Keaton film. Thanks to the commercial and critical success of this new silent film, our uninitiated friends would now be coming along with us to screenings or festivals, or stay up late on Sundays to watch TCM.

They didn't.

The Artist—along with Charles Lane's *Sidewalk Stories* (1989), Mel Brooks's *Silent Movie* (1976), and others—certainly appeared to resemble and behave like a silent movie. As did Pablo Berger's *Blancanieves* (2012), Guy Maddin's *My Winnipeg* (2007), and Andrew Leman's Lovecraft-based *The Call of Cthulhu* (2005). They were referred to as silent movies in their promotional materials and in reviews; the films were told in pantomime; they had wall-to-wall musical scores; they had intertitles. Their releases were met with varying degrees of success.

Just getting financing for a new silent movie must have been a huge uphill battle. Lane's film was made as an independent. Brooks's seemed like its own plot was a meta version of how Brooks got the film made, getting his celebrity friends to make cameos in it. Hazanavicius said at a press screening that I attended that it was not until they hit upon the idea of setting the film in the 1920s, and as a tribute to silent movies, that they were able to get money people on board with the idea of making a new silent.

These films deserve to be better remembered by the moviegoing public who saw them and who are not necessarily silent movie fans—more than as "the one with the little dog...ooh, I loved that dog!" or "the one where Marcel Marceau talks." The people who created and directed these films—Hazanavicius, Brooks, Lane, Berger, and so many others—worked really hard on them.

My money is on the fact that these films come really close to, but just short of, fully inhabiting the Silent Film Universe because of their being filmed at the same speed as the one at which they were to be projected.

Mel Brooks's *Silent Movie* is filmed in real time at 24 fps—except for some of Marty Feldman's slapstick gags—and is in color. The film exists as an unusual hybrid. But Brooks wasn't trying to replicate the medium with his film: "I wanted to do my own concept of a silent movie; I wanted to do my own version. I wanted to *salute* silent movies without actually *doing* a silent movie."[23]

---

[23] Phone conversation between Mel Brooks and filmmaker Lisa Hurwitz (*The Automat*, 2022), who asked Mr. Brooks about this on my behalf, August 13, 2023.

Sidewalk Stories (1989) and *Blancanieves* (2012) are in black and white but are filmed at real-time speed, as are the other new silents I have referenced. *The Artist* was filmed at a slower frame rate, but only very slightly (and without performance tempo adjustments), and so the speed-up is barely noticeable.

At the press screening mentioned above, Hazanavicius said that their research showed that most dramatic films made at the end of the silent era were being cranked at 22 fps, and so they filmed *The Artist* at that frame rate. However, their research was just for cranking speeds but not also projection speeds. Most very late silents were being shown in theaters at 27 fps or faster. If this data had been on their research agenda, a filming speed of 20 fps for projection at the sound standard of 24 fps would have matched the late-1920s speed-up from 22 to 27. And so, the increase in speed from 22 fps to 24 fps in *The Artist* is nearly imperceptible.

I think these "new" silents might have benefited from utilizing the undercranking techniques I have covered here, had they been known of at the time these movies were made. But they weren't—how could they be? I am pretty sure I am the first to have caught on to silent film's utilization of undercranking. My explorations into this phenomenon did not start until around 2008, and my lectures on the topic during the 2010s were for niche audiences—a Chaplin conference in Ohio, the annual Syracuse Cinefest convention, the "Mostly Lost" film identification workshop at the Library of Congress, and MoMA's "To Save and Project" festival of preservation.

The Criterion Collection hired me to do a video essay entitled "A Study in Undercranking" for their 2016 Blu-ray release of Chaplin's *The Kid*. I have made my talk on the subject part of the syllabus for my silent film course at Wesleyan University. I am hoping the publication of this book will generate more awareness of this practice in silent filmmaking.

Armed with a working time machine and the information in the previous chapter, could the filmmakers mentioned above have been able to allow their films to inhabit the Silent Film Universe even more fully? Replacing the real-life state of the physical movement with the altered-reality kind we have observed in vintage silents—which engages our imagination one level further—could very well have imbued these newer silent movies with that ethereal near-dream-state we are so familiar with. This would have allowed these films to more thoroughly resonate with audiences and to become more than a loving tribute or an artistic novelty.

11.

THE FUTURE OF SILENT FILM

So, you want to make a silent movie…

Making a silent movie sounds like a fun idea, right? Over the decades since the silent era, lots of people with movie cameras have done it—home movie enthusiasts, film students, and professionals, shooting on 16mm, 8mm, Super 8mm, and probably also 9.5mm film (the European counterpart to 16mm). They have made their silents either as a novelty, or as die-hard fans paying tribute to the medium they love.

In my teen years as a Super 8 filmmaker, I made a few silent movies. One of them was my attempt at what Keaton had done with multiple exposures in *The Playhouse* (1921). I used a hack I had read about in *Super 8 Filmmaker* magazine to back-wind the film in a Super 8mm cartridge and multiple-expose two or three instances of myself. The record I hit in *Ben Model's Crazy House* (1979) was seven of me waiting in a line to use the bathroom.

My "playhouse" film was shot at 18 fps and shown at 24 fps. Like most Super 8mm cameras, mine had that 18/24 either/or switch on it. My film had carefully made intertitles made with white rub-off letters on black paper. The film was in color. I could have shot in black and

white, as there was Super 8 black-and-white film and processing at the time, and I had filmed another silent short
that way a couple years earlier. I have no recollection of
why I chose color film for the project—perhaps I was not
as aware of what a difference it would make back then.

I loved silent films and wanted to make a movie in
that style. And I did the best I could or was up for, given
what I knew about the medium.

I used the word "tribute" above, and for good reason.

Anyone who has made a silent movie has done so out
of their love for the medium. At best, they are all tributes
to silent cinema and, on a handful of occasions, get really
close to being a silent film. They honor silent movies, are
reminiscent of silent movies, and look a lot like silent
movies—both to the people who made these amateur cinema silents and to the viewers of these films.

I would like to cover here some of the things I keep
seeing done in new silent movies which, it appears, a lot
of people think are facets of silent movies, and just really
are not.

Let's start with the era.

A silent film does not rely on its story taking place in
the 1910s or 1920s. We think of the "look" of silent movies as being culturally *of* those decades. But a 1910s or
1920s setting is not necessary as part of the storytelling
language. It's just that *that* is when the silent movies we
are familiar with were made. But the setting is not what
makes a silent film.

I see this a lot—people dressed in old-style costumes
and hats. Sometimes there are antique automobiles and

other set pieces and props from a century ago. It's not necessary. It may be fun, in a cosplay sort of way, but it's not a requirement for a silent film.

It may also be a faint distraction, unwittingly, to your viewer or audience. They know they are not watching a film from a hundred years ago, after all, and anything that reminds them of this may get in the way of their right-brain experience. Just a little, but it's a factor. An audience or viewer is, in the back of their mind, aware of when a film they are watching was made. No matter how authentic-looking something may appear, we are still cognizant of the fact that it was made decades after the time it is supposed to be from.

The special effects in Woody Allen's *Zelig* (1983) or the black-and-white Hollywood studio look in *Mank* (2020) are remarkable. But when we watch either of these, somewhere in the corner of our consciousness we are aware these are replications done more recently and are not the real thing. Even with the digitally created reel-change cue marks in *Mank*, we are aware that these were generated with a computer, and in the year the film was made. It is because of this unconscious awareness of a film or TV show's time of production that the original *Twilight Zone* episodes still resonate. We *know* we are watching something made during 1959–1964 and that the shows' commentaries are of *that* time, and that is why any "reboot" of the show has to face the challenge of capturing the magic of the original.

I find I keep referencing Charlie Chaplin in my discussions of all this, and I think bringing him up again here is warranted. Chaplin's *Modern Times* is a silent movie, but make no mistake about it—the film takes place in 1936. It may be harder to make the distinction between eras with *City Lights* (1931), since much of it takes place in that Chaplinesque-Dickensian world some of his films inhabit, but if you look at the costumes and automobiles, that film's story takes place in 1931. Chaplin's "post-silent era" silent films take place in the year they were made. So does Yasujiro Ozu's *I Was Born, But...* (1932) and the other silents he made in the 1930s.

If you are interested in trying your hand at silent film, make your silent movie inhabit the world that is concurrent with its production. Your audience will see your silent movie as a culturally contemporaneous movie, just as the silent era's audiences did when they went to the pictures, when silent movies were just called "movies."

• • •

The same standard should be held for storylines and story tropes. As ubiquitous as many typical plots and character archetypes may have been in the silent movies we know, some core aspects of these can still work in a contemporary setting without emulating culture of a hundred years ago.

The conflicts, frustrations, and desires we possess as humans still hold, but the stock plots of a "pretty girl" being flirted with by the male "hero," or a main character getting chased by cops, for example, deserve some updating. Granted, finding a way to make this fit into a film that takes place *now* may not be easy. But holding on to character or story archetypes that contemporary viewers will notice as being from another and very much bygone era may create a barrier—whether conscious or unconscious—and will keep your audience from being absorbed into the world of your silent film.

Scene from *A Day's Messing* (2011), starring and directed by Jeff Seal. Set in contemporary times, the film follows the comic exploits of a bike messenger in New York City on an odyssey to deliver a package.
(courtesy of Jeff Seal)

True, many of these tropes and archetypes may still hold—someone being distracted by an overly attractive person, feeling threatened by someone much bigger or stronger, misunderstanding someone else, and so forth—but the cultural applications these had in the 1920s are not what makes your film a silent film. It is the fact that they are tropes or archetypes easily recognized by viewers without having it all explained in detail in titles. It is the use of visual iconography we are familiar with and can fill in with our imaginations. Why not employ tropes that more easily resonate with today's performers and audiences?

After all, you do want to have the option—if you are so inclined—to cast actors or include principal characters who had little to no agency or were invisible in society during the silent era. Silent film's ability to more universally express stories of the human experience makes it an ideal type of cinema to use for stories whose protagonists are women, people of color, people with disabilities, people who identify as LGBTQAI+, and others who have been historically underrepresented in cinema.

There are costuming possibilities with today's clothing that can meet the needs of silents. For comedies, loose-fitting cargo pants can substitute for baggy clown-vaudeville pants, and Converse sneakers a few sizes too big can stand in for slap shoes. You don't even have to go that far.

Again, look at Chaplin's *Modern Times*. The evil landlord or overbearing mean boss has been replaced by characters from the Industrial Age factory. The President of Electro Steel Corp., played by Allan Garcia, does not wear the Rasputin-like makeup Eric Campbell sports in Chaplin's Mutual comedies. The usual silent era Chaplin late-Victorian house with maid and servant that is broken into as a hideout is here a contemporary department store, where Charlie runs into an old factory buddy. The men in the film wear 1930s fedoras instead of derbies. And on and on.

It is our right-brain experience as an audience, filling in the various aspects of story and character left out as part of the filmmaking and storytelling processes, that is the very reason a 1917 dramatic feature or a 1924 comedy short is still entertaining and accessible today to any audience, of any age, anywhere in the world. If we let go of the culture of the 1920s in making a silent film, and embrace the cinematic aesthetics of silent film, a silent made today can work and appeal on the same level as one made in the silent era.

I think this is the distinction to be considered when the desire is "to avoid doing something museum-y" (an expression several people used when discussing this with me). For cinema's first three decades, the basics of silent film that I have been describing worked just fine and were a universal language for all moving pictures, worldwide. The silent movies we know may have been made in the first third of the last century, but the visual storytelling language they spoke is still a functioning and valid language. It is so because of its use of precisely what anyone with no exposure to silent movies assumes is going to be off-putting: the things that are missing.

The leaving out, the suggestion, the archetypes without deeply explained backstory, the story and location shifts hinted at in a five-word title—these all drew us in to the world of the film, into the universe of silent film, and can still do so.

Granted, bringing silent movies into the twenty-first century may be problematic. We do live in a time when a French-farce plot can be unraveled in five seconds by having the main characters text each other. But the medium of silent film *can* work today. It is worth playing with, and there are new stories and statements about life that can be told, spoken in the universal language of silent film.

• • •

Let's get something straight about silent movie intertitles: like the "old film look" filter on most software and apps, most of what is assumed of or that is turned up in internet searches about silent movie title cards is not what the "real thing" actually looks like. "Old film" and "dust and scratches" filters just make your video or footage look like a film print that has been duped down a few generations and run through classroom projectors by high-school teachers for forty years. But that film when originally made and shown did not possess all that blur, jitter, dirt, and vertical scratches.

Two other assumptions about silent film intertitles— flowery borders and language—can be visual barriers for a contemporary viewer or audience. They are also not from actual silent movies—their origins are in send-ups of silents that were made in the 1930s and 1940s. These "let's poke fun at Grandma's creaky olde-tyme flickers" shorts made and released by major studios set a look and feel for what the general public thinks of when you say "silent film." People making movies and TV commercials in the 1950s and 1960s carried this titling stereotype on.

And so, the ornate and frilly border design—rarely seen, if ever, in actual silents—is assumed to be the look of silent movie titles, and it still is today. Just search for "silent film title background" online and you will see this sort of curlicue-and-ivy border in the first page or two of results, many of which were probably created in the 2010s (the 16:9 aspect ratio is a clue). For examples of the real McCoy, take a trip through any of the social media feeds that post silent film title screen grabs.

The corny, Victorian-sounding prose is another device created for spoofs of silents and should be avoided. The "Unhand me, you villain!" and "Our hero rushes to save Nell from the buzz-saw" language actually derives from the stage melodramas that were antecedents of motion pictures. How this became associated with and became a trope for silent movie titles is beyond me.

You want your title cards to function for your audience of today the way the ones from the silent era did. Those titles employed a set of visual and graphical standards that made reading the titles easy on the eye and brain so that they are part of the film's storytelling flow and not an interruption.

Having made or remade many title cards for my home video releases, always basing their look on frame grabs of existing titles from a particular studio and year, I have observed a consistency of letter size, line spacing, margins, and word count that spans the years of the silent era. The people who have authentically recreated titles for archival restorations as well as those who have worked on my projects agree with this practice and follow the same unwritten rules. There is an economy and often a poetry to the wording in intertitles. They give us just enough information, the word count reduced to a degree that each title card is informative and expressive while allowing us to assume the rest.

Studying and following these formatting rules for intertitles will guide you in the making of the one you or your graphic designer create.[24] You're not just copying a vintage look by doing so. These tenets were used throughout the silent era so that the titles were uniformly visually palatable and accessible to all moviegoers.

• • •

Is it necessary, in making a new silent movie, to use a hand-cranked 35mm motion picture camera? It's fun, I'm sure, and you have the satisfaction of physically replicating what was happening on a shooting stage in the silent era. But it's not a required element of the visual, cinematic language of silent film.

You don't need to use a push mower to cut the grass on your lawn anymore. You can, and it may viscerally connect you with the experience your grandparents or great-grandparents had, but it's not a required piece of machinery for mowing the lawn. In the end, the blades of grass in front of your house are now somewhat uniformly shorter and the same height...which is what you were going for.

What is key, though—regardless of the equipment used—is the ability to adjust your "cranking" speed when taking your scenes. Ideally you want to be able to capture at a frame rate that is slower than that of the playback frame rate. And if you can't capture your video this way, you can use your video editing program to speed up your footage.

---

[24] For a detailed discussion of typefaces, text formatting, wording, backgrounds, and more, go to silentfilmmusic.com/SFUniverse.

Ideally, using a camera or a video-capturing device that allows for the taking of fewer images per second yields the subtle but aesthetically pleasing factor that replicates the look that you get from using a motion picture camera that is either hand-cranked or has a variable-speed electric motor. It's a subtle difference but the overall look is smoother than computer programs or apps that just eliminate a frame or two or three every second to speed-compress the footage.

If you really want to film *on film* and hand-crank your scenes, go for it. In doing so, you will also bring the purr of the running camera to your set, a sound that many silent movie actors missed when the motion picture camera had to be soundproofed for talkies.

And if you are looking for another way to replicate the on-set authenticity of silent era moviemaking, have a musician or two on set to play mood music—just like they did back in the 1920s.

EPILOGUE

I hope this book has been useful, educational, thought-provoking, or food for thought. In providing answers to questions about silent movies that I have been asked many times in interviews, I have tried over and over for years to come up with a simple, concise, and accessible answer for a journalist as to why people in a particular city or town should come to a local theater or museum to see a silent film.

It's not easy.

One of the quotes I throw out to a journalist every time, and which rarely gets used in the published article, is something I frequently hear from people who have come to a silent film show for the first time: "This was way more fun than I thought it was going to be!"

Which is true.

What I have tried to lay out here in *The Silent Film Universe* are my observations and theories about why that first experience with silent movies is more fun than people expect it to be. Because on the surface, these really *really* old movies should not hold up. And yet the reaction the students in my silent film course at Wesleyan University have when seeing Douglas Fairbanks for the first time is always the same. It's very positive, fun, and engaging. And all they are seeing at first—before we move on to watching *The Mark of Zorro* (1920)—is the first twenty-three minutes of Fairbanks's *A Modern Musketeer* (1917).

I may have gotten some of the ideas and concepts and aesthetics wrong, but even with the facets of silent film that are nearly impossible to research, I can't think of any other explanation for some of these elements of silent film. This was the case with my undercranking studies, initially, and over the years some documentary evidence supporting the theories I had devised came to light. I hope the same happens with the other aesthetic concepts and components of the storytelling language of silent cinema that I have laid out in these pages.

You may think I've hit the nail on the head with these ideas and theories, or you may disagree with some or all of them.

But I felt it was important to lay all of this out so that it can be discussed and addressed. There are many, many books on silent film history, on stars and directors and studios and production companies from the "silent era." In writing *The Silent Film Universe*, I wanted to answer the question we all may have for ourselves, and have certainly been asked by our friends, as to why we like silent film. It's a multipronged answer, one with several tributaries and tangents. It's one that is rooted in silent film's unplanned reliance on our unwittingly and unconsciously engaging our imagination, and our right-brain function being activated more so than with regular film, TV, or video.

Silent film is not a dead language. Silent film can still work today.

EPILOGUE

If the films from the silent era still hold up, despite seeming almost completely out of step culturally, new silent film can be made and be similarly entertaining, effective, and enthralling, provided the visual storytelling language of silent film is understood and utilized by anyone making silent movies today.

I'll see you at the silents!

THE SILENT FILM UNIVERSE

For video clips and more visit
silentfilmmusic.com/SFUniverse

photo by Michael Kushner

ABOUT THE AUTHOR

Ben Model is a silent film accompanist, historian, presenter, and educator…although not necessarily in that order. He has spent most of his adult life in the endeavors of promoting silent cinema and preserving the audience for it.

Ben is one of the nation's leading silent film accompanists, and performs on both piano and theatre organ. Over the past four decades he has created and performed thousands of live scores for silent movie screenings.

Ben works full-time as a silent film accompanist. He has been a resident silent film accompanist at the Museum of Modern Art (NY) since 1984 and at the Library of Congress (VA) since 2009, and has presented and accompanied silents at historic theatres, museums, churches, schools, and universities around the USA. He performs regularly at the TCM Classic Film Festival, the Kansas Silent Film Festival, and Capitolfest, and has served as an accompanist for the Syracuse Cinefest, the Fall Cinesation, Slapsticon, the Mostly Lost film identification workshop at the Library of Congress, and the Silent Film Days festival in Tromsø, Norway. He has composed orchestra and concert band scores for silent film shorts that have been performed by professional, university, and high school ensembles around the USA and internationally. Ben has recorded silent film scores for home video releases by Kino Lorber, Milestone Films, ReelclassicDVD, ClassicFlix, Thanhouser Company Film Preservation, Inc., and Undercrank Productions. Many of these have been aired on Turner Classic Movies.

Ben's efforts to program and produce silent film shows include conceiving, launching, and producing the year-round monthly Silent Clowns Film Series in Manhattan in 1997, co-organizing silent film series for the Museum of Modern Art, and co-programming the Anything But Silent series at the Cinema Arts Centre on Long Island since 2006. He expanded this work to the realm of home video, launching the boutique Blu-ray/DVD label Undercrank Productions in 2012 to restore and release unheralded gems of the silent era. Many of these releases were funded by fans through Kickstarter.

Ben utilized live-streaming and D.I.Y. tech during the COVID-19 pandemic to present *The Silent Comedy Watch Party* every week on YouTube, bringing laughter, joy, and relief to viewers around the globe. Throughout the pandemic lockdown, Ben—along with Steve Massa, Susan Selig, Mana Allen, Marlene Weisman, and Crystal Kui—shared more than 250 slapstick comedy shorts, all of them live-accompanied by Ben and live-introduced by Steve. The streams also had as guests renowned silent movie historians and film curators from archives in the USA and overseas. The more than 100 episodes of the show are still available online to view, study, and enjoy.

Ben is a visiting professor of film at Wesleyan University's College of Film and the Moving Image, where he has been teaching (and accompanying) a silent film course since 2015. Ben's *Silent Film Music Podcast*, started in 2012, has allowed him to share his knowledge, techniques, and experience as a silent film accompanist.

Ben has similarly applied his multi-hyphenate skills to the "audience preservation" of pioneering television co-median Ernie Kovacs, serving as both historian and archivist for the Ernie Kovacs and Edie Adams Television Collections. He has curated a career retrospective in the DVD box sets *The Ernie Kovacs Collection: Volume 1*, *The Ernie Kovacs Collection: Volume 2*, and *Take a Good Look – The Definitive Collection* (2011, 2012, and 2017, Shout! Factory), and co-edited the book *Ernie In Kovacsland* (2023, Fantagraphics Books).

He lives in New York City with his family — Mana Allen, Molly Model, and Henry Richey.

website: silentfilmmusic.com
social media: @silentfilmmusic